The Memoirs of an Idiot – In Retrospect

1920-2002

Written by:
Bernard C. Ahouse

ISBN: 978-0-578-09889-0

Throughout man's years-long history
He's oft dwelt on the word "shit"
It's true meaning was usually quite murky
This poem should clarify it

Bullshit is a byproduct
From the making of most cheese
Tis also a quaint expression
Of one's trying to displease.

Horseshit comes in a neater package
As most of us should know
Like the oily words of a salesman
When he's really trying to show.

Chicken shit is a gagging matter
By the Army made renown
Where a smile is easily killed
By a Non-Com's ugly frown.

Ape shit is a romantic notion
That pushes many a man along
Who thinks he's a swinging hero
But is usually a foolish clown.

Tough shit is a hardening period
When we all feel utmost distress.
It was bad enough in days gone by
But much worse since high interest.

No shit is a sidestepping motion
When there is nothing else we can say
It would be nicer to be agreeable
But whoever was born that way?

If after reading this composition
You feel slightly like a fool
Put your thoughts at ease and know
That all shit can be used as a tool.

By Bernard C. Ahouse

Foreword

'Life's but a walking shadow, a poor player that struts and frets his hour upon the stage and then is heard no more. It is a tale told by an idiot, full of sound and fury signifying nothing.' Macbeth, Act 5

Bernard Ahouse was born in 1920 in Nanticoke, PA, one of five children. He also had five stepsiblings. He still has two living sisters, Olga Ahouse Bragg and Mildred Ahouse Tolle.

Bernie is my uncle... well sort of. His wife Irene (often referred to as "Jimmsy") and my father shared the same mother, my Grandmother Tillie. When my dad died suddenly in 1976 at the age of 56, and my mother became institutionalized as a result of my dad's death. I quietly adopted Bernie and Irene as my surrogate mom and dad. I have always loved them both equally, and they have always helped me to feel a part of their family. Irene never ever forgot my birthday.

They raised four children—Karl, Susan, Nancy and Martin—and lived near the village of Lodi, NY for more than 60 years. Though once a large, thriving productive farm of more than 1,000 acres, today all that remains is the old farmhouse, a lone silo from the barn that burned down many years ago, about 20 acres surrounding the house, and so many memories. The balance of the farm is now a part of the Finger Lakes National Forrest.

Irene died peacefully at home a little more than a year ago after a very long illness. We all miss her.

Martin lives with his wife Becky and their children, Joe and Alana, in the home that Martin built very near the old farmhouse in Lodi on land that had been part of the original farm. Nancy lives in the neighboring town of Ovid, while Susan now makes her home in Belize. Sadly, Karl died shortly after Irene. There are nine grandchildren, who have a dream of preserving the old farmhouse for their posterity. Bernie is also blessed with three great-grandchildren—Liam, Jack and Will.

When Bernie became an octogenarian, he began to write down random remembrances and opinions of times and events in his life, mostly based on volumes of notes that he kept. Throughout his life, he actually maintained a detailed log of every business-related phone call he ever made or received! Beginning on Oct. 23rd 2000, he wrote these memoirs until June 20th 2002.

Susan's daughter Emily transcribed the bulk of the pages, but her sister Lisa also did a number of them as well. It is incomplete at 366 entries, as there are a total of 488 written. Their monumental task was one of love and patience, as Bernie's handwritten script became almost impossible to read. Without their hard work, this would never have made it to print. Susan was able to provide us with the photographs for both covers and the insert.

Bernie Ahouse chose the title *Memoirs of an Idiot – In Retrospect* for this volume. If Shakespeare is indeed Bernie's inspiration, Bernie would find that many disagree with this choice on several levels. We may understand the "struts and fret's" and "sound and fury" from his younger days, but "signifying nothing" is not consistent with the facts. Bernie Ahouse was involved in many varied schemes and transactions during his lifetime, about which he took copious and detailed notes.*

For a "farmer from upstate New York", Bernie Ahouse was involved with people and events on both a local and national level that would surprise anyone who didn't know him. The details of many of these events add heretofore-unavailable insights into major events with which we are all familiar. Some of the tales in this book highlight Bernie's keen eye for coincidence. These experiences would have escaped most of us, just because we failed to ask ourselves what was possible.

Family and friends who have heard most of these stories, often more than once, will tell you that they seem to always begin "did I tell you about the time…?" Sometimes at the end of a story, I have had to question the verity of his tale. The answer is easy. How could anyone make this stuff up?

We hope you enjoy Bernie's memoir, published in celebration of his 90th birthday!

*Bernie not only kept detailed notes of his telephone conversations, he has stored copies of manuscripts, deeds, photographs, newspaper articles and court proceeding to document his experiences. His office is filled with files and logs on his dealings. He also maintains every cancelled check he ever wrote!

#1 – Monday October 23, 2000

The purpose of these memoirs is not to, necessarily, provide substance for a novel, but to record an insight into the happenings in my lifetime that may be important, interesting, or humorous. I will name names as I recall with no intent to be malicious. I have no bone to pick with any individual, but some groups may appear to be treated otherwise. I believe my mind is clear and my memory is as good as ever. And, I pray, that I live long enough to set all facts and matters down.

— B.C. Ahouse

#2 – Tuesday October 24, 2000

I am now an octogenarian, having past my 80 years last April 25, 2000. As to what is my nature and character, I believe I best described myself to a lawyer some years ago as a pragmatic altruist. I don't think the illiterate "proscriptor" knew what I said. On reflecting on his stupidity, I plainly stated that I always tried to see all the facets of any situation and to do the best for all concerned within my ability. I am not a liar, as the word is commonly understood; but I realize that I don't indulge in talking unnecessarily. I will never stand aside if I can prevent an injustice or abuse to any one or thing.

— B.C. Ahouse

#3 – Wednesday October 25, 2000

I wish to reflect on an incident that occurred while Irene, my wife, was in the Intensive Care department in Geneva Hospital. I was asked into the office of a Ms. McCarthy, their Social Services expert. She mentioned her knowledge of Irene and I enjoying an evening martini daily and suggested it was the cause of Irene's problem. I disagreed and mentioned that it was legal. A few nights later while I was home, she called about at two a.m. stating that it was Geneva Hospital, which frightened me. She then said she hoped I didn't have a martini. She also had her subordinates dun me. The following May, in 1995, she was murdered in Rochester in the middle of the night by a person who knew she carried a large sum of money to buy cocaine for her group. This all came out later in court and the killer was convicted.

— B.C. Ahouse

#4 – Friday October 27, 2000

I have often been asked why I never became active in sports while in high school. I once did go out for football, an episode which ended when I returned an unwelcome punch from a fellow student player. The real matter was that I was the sole supplier of heat for our home (coal). I would run home after school (about one mile) to be early on the Culm Bank, where I and many competitors waited at the dumping end of this huge pile at Bliss Colliery. I bagged as much as I could carry and hauled it home in a coaster wagon. Sometimes I would venture to the shaft head of Auchin Claus Colliery or into hole from the face, but the Coal and Iron Police made this too risky.

— B.C. Ahouse

#5 – Saturday October 28, 2000

I am a person who is very slow to judge another or a situation. Sometimes, when I finally do it, it's often mistaken for a change of opinion. I chaired the Seneca County Conservation Board for many years and on a few occasions, my decisions were viewed as a change of attitude. I have decided, though, that it is to the benefit of all to not be hasty in such matters. On occasions when the board voted on a matter, I endorsed their decision with my signature.

—B.C. Ahouse

#6 – Sunday October 29, 2000

About 20 years ago, we were in Milwaukee with Irene's sister Peggy and her husband Tom; he was on company business, and I was there to visit a business associate, Bill Pousoldt, at his plant. We dropped Tom off at his plant, and Peg drove Irene and me to a shopping mall. The plan being that they would set up there, and I would go on my way. We all got out of the car with it running and quickly locked all the doors! I suggested I went to a store to get a coat hanger, hoping to grab hold of the lock inside the car. Poor luck. A little old lady approached me, called me "Sonny" and asked if she could help us in our troubles. I said sure if she could, whereupon, she took a chrome-plated hook out of her car, inserted it in the vent, unlatched the lock, and opened the door. All true.

— B.C. Ahouse

#7 – Monday October 30, 2000

About 20 years ago, I was in a plane from NYC to Syracuse and struck up a conversation with a tall black man from Dakar by the name of Ibraham Mohamed. I asked him what was new in Senegal, and he said woman's lib. I queried him about it. He replied that his religion allowed him four wives. But it was now necessary to get proper license from the magistrate. The first question on the form was, "Do you intend to marry again?" If you said yes, the first wife promptly left you. If you said no but did, the wife could obtain title to your property and a divorce. Obviously, he didn't like woman's lib.

— B.C. Ahouse

#8 – Monday October 30, 2000

Regarding my wife Irene's mistreatment in the Geneva General Hospital:

The Health Department of New York State condemned them for malpractice. However, they must have fabricated some additional information. I don't know what they said but I rely on Dr. Fred Fett's statement that he was astonished that anything like their actions could have happened. I note this at this time after coming upon the misplaced letter.

—B.C. Ahouse

#9 – Tuesday October 31, 2000

Twenty-some years ago, a farmer named Bill Bennet said he was referred by Harry Harkuss (a good guy) to buy hay from us. Harry said to make sure he had the money to pay. I called the Troy National Bank in Pennsylvania that he mentioned. The bank said he had money for six loads of hay. We delivered six to him, and he paid with six checks that I systematically deposited in my bank about three months later. They were all bounced because of insufficient funds. I went right to the bank in Troy, Pennsylvania, and I asked to speak to the cashier, who came right out, heard my complaint, and told me that I should be a more astute businessman. I asked to use his phone. He asked why. I stated to call the state police. He asked why. I stated to report a bank robbery. He immediately came up with the cash for me.

— B.C. Ahouse

#10 – Wednesday November 1, 2000

Some 40 or 50 years ago in some heated discussions with young Jimmy Rand, I challenged him to develop a method to enable a blind person to see, mainly by electrical impulse, which I thought of as the means of transferring light to the brain. He dismissed my theory, saying that it was chemical. Early this year, several articles appeared in the *Finger Lakes Times* supporting my thoughts. I have been advised to send the letter to the paper, but I am a little disturbed by the situation.

– B.C. Ahouse

#11 – Thursday November 2, 2000

I have never campaigned for any political person or party, but I thought I'd including the attached document, which I copied after receiving it from my son Martin. I decided it was something for posterity. I have always said that Bill Clinton is proof that anybody can be president. I also saw a newspaper article about Rob Van Vleet, which was a surprise to me, his being a Democrat. My opinion is that either vice president would be a better president than those nominated.

— B.C. Ahouse

#12 – Friday November 3, 2000

When I was stationed at Mitchell Field for a while with the United States Engineer Department out of 120 White Hall Building, Wall St. The first K-9 dogs were brought into the Army. I happened by a fenced enclosure where a well-padded sergeant was beginning a training period with two large Doberman Pinscher dogs. He was taking his time, which annoyed a major (of smaller stature) who told the sergeant to step aside so he could show him how to operate. The sergeant did and the major stepped in. The two dogs immediately nailed him to the ground and chewed him up. I asked the sarge to interfere. He said, "No, the major is showing me how to do my job."

—B.C. Ahouse

#13 – Saturday November 4, 2000

In the Summer of 1943, we were marching in close formation in a suburban area of Fort Belvoir—Lt Rey and I were on point. It was a very hot day and everybody felt it. As we approached an intersection, a very attractive young woman raised her hand in recognition and slowly passed out and fell to the pavement. Lt. Rey and I went to her assistance. She was barely breathing and was extremely hot. Her pulse was weak, and we noticed that the tight girdle she was wearing was obstructing her breathing. Naturally we did as we saw best and removed it. When she finally came to after our helping her, she appeared thankful and embarrassed.

—B.C. Ahouse

#14 – Sunday November 5, 2000

Some 40 years ago, I was in the ocean swimming in Lake Worth, Florida with my children. Everyone was enjoying it until I unexpectedly had a Portuguese man of war (a jelly fish) wrap its long tentacles around my left leg. The sting was noticeable at once, so we left for my mother-n-law's home on D Street. When I got there, my stomach was starting to harden and ache. We called a doctor, who ordered me right in. Immediately he gave me a large shot of Gamma Globulin, which was a relief. I asked him if it was serious. He said I probably had half an hour left when I came in. Incidentally, my left leg is the one that today gives me serious aches and pains.

—B.C. Ahouse

#15 – Monday November 6, 2000

While visiting my in-laws on D Street in Lake Worth, my mother-in-law, Tillie, answered a call which upset her at once. I asked the problem, she said that it was some nut. I took the phone and asked what he wanted. He said to kill somebody. Since there had been two murders recently on the military trail to the west, two miles away, I gave the phone to my wife, Irene, who kept him on the line for about a half-hour by listening to his crude pornography. I went next door and called the police, who traced the call. An officer picked me up and I saw them arrest a fella name Charles Whitman, whose father was a prominent businessman in Lake Worth. I didn't see him again, but after I left, I remembered his name and a short time later recognized him as the sharp shooter who killed twelve people from the Texas Tower Building.

—B.C. Ahouse

#16 – Monday November 6, 2000

To follow up on my comments about Charles Whitman: The following year, after the Dallas massacre, I was again in the Lake Worth, Florida area and visited the police station asking to see the officer I met the previous year. When asked why, I said I wanted to update myself on the happenings I witnessed regarding Charles Whitman. The chief told me this: If I felt good when I got up that day, to leave well enough alone. Recently I became aware that an adjuster, Ken Bohman, and our vice sheriff, Peter, were in Whitman's squad in the Marine Corps. and Bohman said Whitman's theory on life was that you were not a man until you had killed someone.

— B.C. Ahouse

#17 – Tuesday November 7, 2000
Election Day

About ten years ago, while examining some gas and oil leases located in Dederidge County, West Virginia, I noted two in the name of Ahouse and Crest Ahouse. I called the telephone operator in West Virginia and asked for an Ahouse number. She said I must want to talk to Eunice Ahouse, whose number she gave me. I called and she asked who was calling. I said Bernard Ahouse. I heard the phone drop and probably her also. Sometime later her son, Henry, spoke, asking my name and what I was trying to do. I said simply, "To make your acquaintance. What's the problem?"

He said, "My father was Bernard Ahouse and we just buried him."

This caused quite a controversy as related to me by a Mr. Halleran a year later when he noticed my nametag at the Belvoir, NY Oil Men's picnic.

— B.C. Ahouse

#18 – Wednesday November 8, 2000

To follow up on the acquaintances with the Ahouses of West Virginia, my Grandfather Joseph Ahouse and his brother Bernard Ahouse immigrated to the USA after the Franco-Prussian War in 1873. Joseph in Pennsylvania and Bernard going to Colorado, each to labor in coalmines. Bernard eventually relocated to West Virginia, hence his progeny there. This situation caused me to recollect an incident from probably 30 years ago. My brother-in-law, Joseph Brieker of Baltimore, Maryland mentioned me about a Bernard Ahouse being published as an heir to a man who was a renowned *** . I paid no attention to it, probably thinking it was a joke. This now caused me to reflect on it, but I took no action. Incidentally, I recollect helping a florist who worked with me in Ft. Holabird in 1940-41 as a carpenter, which he was not, but I befriended him.

— B.C. Ahouse

#19 – Thursday November 9, 2000

Some 30 or so years ago, while on a chartered fishing boat near Bimini in the Gulf Stream, my son Martin called my attention to an enormous hammerhead shark paralleling the boat. His head was as big as a railroad tie. A sudden thunderstorm came up and unbelievably it thundered a flock of wren-like birds into the water. The fish immediately began feasting on these. One small bird landed on the deck. I picked it up, blew breath into its mouth and slightly revived it. I put it in my shirt pocket, where it recovered. Upon reaching shore, I took it out and placed it on my hand. It gave me one quick look and took off over the open sea.

— B.C. Ahouse

#20 – Friday November 10, 2000

Lake Worth, Florida

Some 30 to 40 years ago, I painted the home exterior for a Ms. Meyer—a sister of Floyd Gibbong, the reknown world correspondent, and the predecessor to Lowell Thomas in fame. Ms. Meyer was a friend of my mother-in-law, Tillie Olson, and I wouldn't accept compensation since it helped me pass the time while on vacation. I did accept a pocket watch. A Hamilton which she said was the one Mr. Gibbous carried on his Sahara Desert Excursion to Timbuktu, I also accepted a book about him. As a humorous slant, she quoted the following ditty of her brother's:

> *Tim and I a wandering went*
> *We spied 3 maidens in a tent*
> *They were 3 and we but 2*
> *So I bucked One*
> *And Tim Bucked Two…*

> —B.C. Ahouse

#21 – Saturday November 11, 2000

Today being Veteran's Day, I wish to reflect on a few events from the past. In 1926, on the Susquehanna River in Wilkes Barre, Pennsylvania, as part of the celebration a boat full of flowers was set adrift and then destroyed by a 75-artillery piece—the 109 Field Artillery being just across the river. Some years later as a boy scout, I was in a parade in Nanticoke, Pennsylvania. We came to a halt in front of the 109 FA Armory on lower Broadway Street. A bus approaching us driven by an enraged operator didn't slow down and ran into the rear of the formation. I recall one boy having his legs crushed. I was not hurt.

—B.C. Ahouse

#22 – Saturday November 11, 2000

For years on NBC nightly news, I watched their logo of the Earth revolving in the wrong direction from East to West. After finally giving up hope that they would correct their error, I phoned to alert them of their mistake. I also wrote them, and almost immediately the Earth changed direction; but they never acknowledged my contribution. Some years later, I mentioned this to Rush Limbaugh, but he never gave me the time of day.

— B.C. Ahouse

#23 – Sunday November 12, 2000

In 1977, because of the bad crop year 1976, I listed the farm, a thousand-plus acres, with Harris Beach and Wilcox through their agent John Townsend of Lodi, New York (also my neighbor). He provided an option to buy from a Bill Balderston and had a check from Bill for $10,000, which Townsend kept. I did not know at the time that the moment (state law) I signed the option, the check was mine. Balderston did not exercise his option, but Townsend kept the check. I don't know what he did with it. In good faith, Irene and I went to Delaware to look at some hundred-acre farmland that Balderston might have used in exchange. I visited with his attorney in Centreville, Maryland. Bob Herrick of Tompkins County Trust Co. has implied that I was defrauded.

— B.C. Ahouse

#24 – Monday November 13, 2000

The evening of the day that Bally's Casino opened in Atlantic City, I drew a blank and also noticed that no one else had any luck on the slots. A security guard overheard my conversation with another fellow called Bin Ali and invited me upstairs for a drink. He introduced me to a fellow who he said was Nat King Cole's brother. I had a couple of martinis with them, which affected me more than I ever knew. I barely made it back to Caesar's, where I was staying. The next day I had a hang over, the only one in my life before or since.

—B.C. Ahouse

#25 – Monday November 13, 2000

Back in the early 1960s, my father-in-law Adolph Lentz passed away. He had recently purchased a 1960 Rambler Sedan and financed it with Marine Midland in Elmira and got the signer insurance, which covered the unpaid balance on the sales contract. The bank sent my wife Irene (the heiress) the paid contract and title to the car. I was aware of NY State Installment Clause. I assumed that the unearned interest was not the bank's because it was covered by the insurance contract. I suggested that they cut a check for Irene. I visited the bank's loan officer, John Mantanley, who laughed while showing me the compiled file of such interest, which was over a million dollars. I said fine, but cut me a check. They referred me to their law firm in Buffalo (Kohler and Kohler), who agreed with me, and the bank sent the check. I should have done this through Prudential.

— B.C. Ahouse

#26 – Monday November 13, 2000

A poetic response to the well-paid environmentalists:

The putrid mind of the devil
Festered with evil delights

His comrades gathered around him
And they organized animal rights

This quickly excited the Congress
Who with half of their wits

Enacted the Endangered Species mess
Proving themselves sick idiots

Then the environmentalists trotted out
Their slick vocal farters

To champion the rights and fates
Of the little snail darters

To look wholesome to all they
Who call themselves green

Which is falsely said
The truthful fact
Is that they are red.

At the bottom of the pit of the human species,
Squirms the queer group with a taste for feces.

—B.C. Ahouse

#27 – Tuesday November 14, 2000

Forty-some years ago, I took our family to visit the Glass Museum in Corning, New York. After the exhibition, the greatest of which was the failed casting of a huge telescope lens, we visited the gift store. My son Martin, three or four years of age, was interested enough to pick up a Steuben Crystal ashtray. The store manager, in an aggravating fashion, hurried over to chastise him. He then turned to me and said if the boy broke it, there would be much trouble – I agreed, especially if he cut himself on the pieces of the wantonly displayed item.

– B.C. Ahouse

#28 – Wednesday November 15, 2000

During the 1930s, we had a miniature war in Pennsylvania—particularly in Nanticoke. We used to lie in bed and count the explosions of front porches being blown up. The Anthracite coal minters got sick and tired of the United Mine Workers of John Lewis, who were starting the CIO in Detroit. I made my first $5.00 with a bucket of bolts, handed to me by the breaker boss of Susquehanna Coal Co. #7. "Just throw them," he said. There were street fights between the strikers and those who had to work the mine. I recall them taunting a friend, Fred Blythe, as he drove by in his Model T Ford.

"We'll get you later, Fred."

Fred stopped, got out, and went over to the loudmouth saying, "I never go to bed worrying." He then punched the guy in the face. I heard the bones crack from across the street.

—B.C. Ahouse

#29 – Thursday November 16, 2000

The Anthracite Miners Union was organized by a John Maloney. He was a brother-in-law to my mother's (Edith Ahouse) cousin—his wife being Margaret Maloney Hess, and he being Billy Hess. Billy Hess had some administration job with Glen Alden Coal Company. I recall some discussion about the little civil war we had going. There was a fight on Middle Road on the road leading into the college. The news began filming it. The fight stopped, turning against the newsmen and their film equipment. John Maloney and his son were killed by a bomb in a cigar box opened in their home. John's daughter, who I knew, was badly injured and had her breast removed because of splinters. She was a pretty girl. Maloney's brother-in-law (I believe his name to be John Fuggman) was accused, tried, convicted, and executed in the electric chair. This trial sort of paralleled the Bruno Hauptman trial, both were German immigrants. The feeling, I recall, was that Fuggman was not necessarily guilty.

—B.C. Ahouse

#30 – Friday November 17, 2000

To contribute to my mother's (Edith Ahouse) well-being, I forced a resolution to my grandmother's (Lena Brush Burman) estate by having my mother quit her claim to me. I filed it in CH in Wilkes Barre, Pennsylvania and immediately got billed for the back taxes, which I paid. I couldn't settle it amicably, so I retained an old neighbor, Bernard Kotulak, as my attorney. My first cousin, Carl Brush, retained a Mr. Flanagan to represent him. Everything was settled at the courthouse. Getting late in the day, Mr. Flanagan invited me, my wife Irene, and Bruno Kotulak to be his guests at dinner. The conversation led to Mr. Flanagan almost boasting that he had paid the parents of a Ms. Kopekney $200,000.00 to get them not to allow her body to be examined to check for pregnancy at the behest of Senator Ted Kennedy.

— B.C. Ahouse

#31 – Friday November 17, 2000

About 30-some years ago, the Telephone Co of Prattsburg entered on my property and buried a telephone cable without my permission. In doing so, they destroyed the outlets of several tile drainage systems. I asked them to repair them, they refused. I accused them of trespass. They said they had the rights from the Highway Department. I researched this at the law library and discovered that a highway right of way was only for structures relating to the highway. They laughed at this and the told me to sue. I spoke to Henry Koch, who laughed also. I finally retained a young John Sipos, who took it to court and to his surprise won the case—setting a precedent. We were awarded about $2000.00. On another farm, there was a repeat case and another payment to me. Real estate people were amazed.

—B.C. Ahouse

#32 – Friday November 17, 2000

The telephone company always demanded the last cent in their business. At one point, I received a monthly bill for about $600.00. I protested this and sent them a check for $300.00, which they returned and cut off my phone service. I was without service for more than a year. Finally, I got the attention of the New York State Public Service Commission and showed up at a hearing in Albany. The judge was Mike Bayre, who conducted the hearing. A Mr. Wagner V.P. of E, an engineer, and two lawyers pressed their claim against me, who stood there alone. Mr. Bayre examined the list of calls and had an assistant double check, especially the rates and codes for all calls. The result was that I owed Empire about $150.00, which I agreed to pay. After some stammering, the company agreed. Mr. Bayre then told them to restore my service on my terms or give up their franchise.

—B.C. Ahouse

#33 – Friday November 17, 2000

In 1946, shortly after locating on our farm in Lodi, NY, which is presently still our home, I made the acquaintance of a Thaddeus Covert. I was told that he was standing next to President McKinley when he was shot in Buffalo, New York. In one of our discussions, he asked me if I noticed a lot of dumb people in this locality. I said I wouldn't dispute that. He then ventured to tell me why. During the Civil War, a lot of local farmers made a lot of money selling oats and Timothy hay to the Union Army. They then sent their children away to college. The smart ones, almost as a whole, stayed away. The dumb ones returned and continued to produce more dummies.

—B.C. Ahouse

#34 – Friday November 17, 2000

About 20 years ago, my sons Martin and Karl were making arrangements with an agent to have a Woodstock II Concert on our farm property. It all seemed logical to me, so I agreed. Many things happened because of this, but the one that meant most to me was that my insurance was cancelled by my carrier in Trumansburg. I obtained other insurance and asked for a refund of my paid premium. They referred me to another attorney, a new person to me — a Martin A. Luster. He came here from New York City. Upon entering his office, I introduced myself. He loudly said, "Why, you don't have horns!"

I said, "I do, you just don't see them."

John Sipor threatened to sue and they paid, but it cost me a third to John Sipor, who is now Tompkins County State Assemblyman.

— B.C. Ahouse

#35 – Saturday November 18, 2000

In 1974, Irene and I visited the family of Joe Fingerling, whom Irene had met on her trip to Europe the previous year. Joe gave us a tour of the town— Oral Roberts University and his ranch north of town. Also the ancient oil fields and remains. At his ranch house, he served us a can of good beer. As I enjoyed it, his large German shepherd dog sat down in front of me and looked longingly at my can. Joe said when I had finished to give it to him, which I did. The dog chewed on it until he had it down about the size of a chicken egg. He then went over to a gully bank and spit it out. I followed him. The scene looked like a truckload had been dumped there.

— B.C. Ahouse

#36 – Saturday November 18, 2000

Lodi

About 40 some years ago, a group of farmers from Cayuga appeared here asking me to sign a petition to put the Conservative Party on the State Ballot. I agreed with their breed so I did. Some time a little later, my attorney friend Charles Jennings of Lodi, who was then Secretary of the State land board, came to me with a retraction statement. I said, "Chuck, don't tell me what I should do or think." He said that he was only trying to save me a lot of trouble with the State tax department. I took his advice and signed. However, I had substantial trouble with the Farmers Claim Motor Fuel Refund. Complements of Nelson Rockefeller, who cashed my money.

— B.C. Ahouse

#37 – Saturday November 18, 2000

While at a conservation convention in Denver in 1975, Irene and I were having a dinner discussion with John "Dick" Shield and his wife Mildred. Dick was the chairman of the State Democratic Party in Iowa. He was a confidant of LB Johnson, who often lamented his regrets about fellows John Kennedy led into Vietnam. Dick nonchalantly told us that the next president was going to be Georgia's Governor Jimmy Carter. I said I never heard of him and why? Dick said simply because David Rockefeller wanted him. This happened. A while later, Irene and I happened to reflect on this while dining out north of Ithaca, New York. A group of men sitting near overheard us. They introduced themselves as the John Society of Ithaca and invited us in. I refused.

— B.C. Ahouse

#38 – Saturday November 18, 2000

The first lawsuit I was involved in was with Agway, which was formed by uniting GLF Eastern States and the Farm Bureau of Pennsylvania. Since Agway members held one share of common stock, that was it. Since the others didn't, they received stock shares compensatory to their share of retained margins. GLF retainers were in the 585 millions of dollars. Henry Koch induced me to be the plaintiff in resolving this matter at no cost to me. The matter dragged on as is usual until I was told by Henry that the action was dropped. He finally explained to me that Gould had financed his action, and since he got what he wanted by Agway paying a large bill to Gould for pumps receivable, he had no reason to go on.

— B.C. Ahouse

#39 – Saturday November 19, 2000

About 20 years ago, a native of New York City, Ervin Berlin, who lived formerly in Texas, bought a farm in Cayuga County and asked me to fly to New York City. I did not know why until I got to the law offices of Curtis Mallet, who I was told were representing John Mitchell—Nixon's man in his problems. The task I was presented with was to renew my lawsuit against Agway regarding the retainer margins (which at this point today have practically disappeared). This was at the behest of Bella Absugy, who thought it would favor her in her bid to replace Jacob as U.S. senator. After consideration, I refused and was then escorted through the three-story office and to dinner. In one hallway was a box with 20 feet of butcher paper that looked like someone had cleaned their paint brushes on it. I asked if it was real? She said she hoped so as the old man had paid $10,000 for it.

– B.C. Ahouse

#40 – Sunday November 19, 2000

Later, while at Curtis Mallet's law offices, a Lars Engahahl brought up the matter regarding Equitable Real Estate Trust—a matter they were litigating. I happened to remark that they were going south on some occasion (I don't know how they were aware of this). I recalled saying it at a meeting with Amory Houghton of Corning Glass regarding a building proposition. They interested me in the Virgin Islands, U.S. I traveled to Lake Worth, Florida, in particular to speak to a familiar builder in that area. He told me to forget it because of Equitable being finished. He asked me if I could fix the date. I said certainly. By my gas credit charges across the country, it appeared that I was aware of this situation before. The auditing firm being charged maintained they knew of the matter, which was probably covered up. I gave a statement of such without recompense.

—B.C. Ahouse

#41 – Sunday, November 19, 2000

Chief Executive Officer
Nabisco
East Hanover, N.J. 07936

Dear Sir:

I have an original print in excellent condition, signed by N.C. Wyeth, and dated '06. I enclose a photo which shows a glare caused by the Plexiglas cover. The caption on the bottom simply says, "Where the Mail Goes, Cream of Wheat Goes". Perhaps you may be interested in obtaining it for Nabisco Archives.

With Thanks,
Respectfully Yours,
Bernard Ahouse

#42 – Sunday November 19, 2000

About 15 years ago, we stopped at Jekyll Island, Georgia and stayed at a Holiday Inn. I asked the clerk when the dining room opened and he said, "5:00 a.m." — nothing more. When Irene and I showed up there, the hostess wouldn't seat us because we had no reservation. The place was empty. We went up the coast a mile or so and found a seafood smorgasbord — the best I ever enjoyed. The next day I thanked the hostess for not seating us. The next day I went out on the beach with my metal detector — the only other person in sight was a man coming south who waved and we made contact. I asked him where he was from. He said Petersboro, Ontario, Did I know of it? I said yes, I sold oats to out there. He asked who I dealt with. I happened to recall and mention his name. He said, "Well, shake his hand."

— B.C. Ahouse

#43 – Monday November 20, 2000

In the mid 1970s, while driving through Houston's south side, I noticed a place of business sign that rang a bell. Some years ago, my young son Martin had sent $35.00 to a similar address to buy a metal detector which he never received. As best I could, I explained it to a fellow inside. He said he didn't doubt it one bit, that he had recently bought the business from a poor operator. He said he definitely wanted to make it right and told me to take my pick from a large selection in the rear of the store. I said I had no idea which to choose to make it right. He picked out a Beachcomber Induction Balance Detector (which we still have and is in mint condition). I said, "Hey, that's priced at $125.00. I'll pay you the difference."

He said, "No way. I'm pleased to right a wrong with a man."

— B.C. Ahouse

#44 – Monday November 20, 2000

One time during the 1970s, a friend and rancher — a fellow conservationist—was showing us around his property. Having mentioned the pecans grown locally, he said he would show me a pecan harvester a friend had designed. It was a truck with two sawbucks which supported a large log (about 24 inches in diameter and 12 feet long). The front end was padded with layers of tire rubber. He simply drove into the tree and the pecans fell to the ground. On the return trip, we stopped at a six-acre stand of locust trees. The wild turkeys in it were beyond count. My wife, Irene, couldn't believe they were wild. But what a sight when Fred tooted the horn and several hundred took flight toward a similar stand in the distance.

—B.C. Ahouse

#45 – Monday November 20, 2000

A mutual friend of mine said of Bud Tucker of Jet, Oklahoma: "You know it isn't a big bank, but it's all Bud's." On one occasion, I was to meet Bud in the bank and go out for lunch at a cattleman's club on the Salt River. Bud said he had to wait for a customer who soon came in. He asked Bud if he had the money, and Bud handed him fifty, one-hundred-dollar bills. He signed a note and left. I said that was a quick deal. Bud said yes. He was going to Las Vegas and needed some walking around money. I was surprised upon returning to New York. I went to the Wheeler Bank in Interlaken, which was being reorganized by a Warren Koehler from Philadelphia. Warren asked me what was on my mind. I said I wanted $5000.00. He said why? I said I was going to Las Vegas. Warren looked at me and couldn't even speak or spit.

— B.C. Ahouse

#46 – Monday November 20, 2000

A conservation friend, John Wilder, who was also the Speaker of the Tennessee Senate, was quite a storyteller, and I want to record some as I remember them. His father, a banker in, I believe, Sommersville, Tennessee had a friend who lost his wife after 50 years of marriage. The old fellow, in his late seventies, after a proper mourning period married a lady in her fifties. They got along fine for a little while, but then they ran into some stormy weather. The old boy began to wander and his new wife was told about it. At first, she didn't believe it. When she did, she held her tongue, but she soon became angry and then furious, tracking him down to a motel with a lady in her seventies. In desperation, she asked, "What in the world does she have that I haven't?"

The old boy replied, "Just one thing, patience."

—B.C. Ahouse

#47 – Monday November 20, 2000

About 1978, while working in Washington on business with the Forest Service, Philip Thornton asked me if I had time to go over to the Justice Department to meet Griffin Bell—Attorney General Bell. Upon making his acquaintance, he told me of the Cayuga Indians land claim, which he said would not be won in court and about the Memorandum of Understanding which he would like me to verbally deliver to the Seneca County Board of Supervisors. I recall it was for $8,500,000.00 and a land award of, I believe, 1,600 acres. I was at that time chairing the Seneca Conservation Board and they brought it to the board's attention, including two member supervisors, Larry Wilkery and James Somerville, who immediately flared up at me saying he was sick and tired of my bringing bad news to Seneca. This started Wisner Kinne PhD on his tirade.

— B.C. Ahouse

#48 – Monday November 20, 2000

I wish to note the accomplishments of my nephew, Gary Ahouse's son, Alex Ahouse. Alex was a good athlete at South Seneca School and an extraordinary student. Because of his scholastic standing, he was awarded a full scholarship at Hobart College in Geneva, NY. As I was told, this amounts to $25,000.00 tuition for four years and also some subsistence cash. I do not know of his being involved in sports there. This is his first year. I understand that he is doing well.

— B.C. Ahouse

#49 – Tuesday November 21, 2000

While chairing the Seneca County Conversation Board in the mid-1970s, I was instrumental in hiring Wayne Brewer. His first job on conservation work was as a technician. This was instrumental in his getting appointed as a game warden. I was also on the first Wildlife Board Avon, NY. I spoke to Captain Frank Ely, who said that Wayne was too short. His brother, Martin, has told me that Wayne used to hang by his heels to stretch out. With some help, he got the job he wanted. I understand he made a drug bust which may have been responsible for his being transferred to the Fish (Fulton) Market in New York City, where I heard he had some mob problems, may have even used his gun. Anyway, his perseverance stood the test and he advanced to mayor. He recently retired. Although I know his mother Rose, brother Marty, and his sister, I have never met Wayne Brewer in person.

— B.C. Ahouse

#50 – Tuesday November 21, 2000

About 1985 – John Block at Rules and Regulations Meeting in Syracuse, New York.

Throughout the 39 years that I have been a farmer in Seneca County, New York, I have watched a wide variety of federal agricultural programs go by. With the exception of Soil and Water Conservation, the present sad state of affairs must label the bulk of them a failure.

It isn't that much good thought hasn't been given to a solution, but that priorities other than agriculture's economic strength have been foremost. Cheap food has consistently been every administration's goal. If food was given equal cost status, with housing for example, agriculture's economics could be improved.

I would suggest that the most logical way of doing this would be through marketing quotas. I accept the fact that the government isn't going to get out of agriculture, and I believe the bureaucracy is capable of properly apportioning these quotas. Quotas would total all necessary volume for a healthy economy. Values would be costed by a "General Motors" or a "Teamsters Union" formula.

Any surplus produced by any individual farm, should remain on that farm and be the responsibility of the producer, not the government or any corporation. A farmer with filling storage would not be tempted to overproduce.

I am certain that many interest groups would immediately protest, but I hope what we are doing here is to benefit agriculture. Needless to say, nothing will matter unless some Legislative action is taken to restore the usury rate of interest to what is was before; when Secretary Earl Butz thought he could start agriculture on the road to lasting prosperity.

—B.C. Ahouse

John Block asked me to address the Rules and Regulations Meeting—he agreed with me but said it would never fly.

#51 – Wednesday November 22, 2000

Fred Williams graduated with me from Nanticoke High School in 1938. My only physical contact with him was when we were young teenagers. Fred's father put us together on Maple Street in Washington and told us to fight. He must have wanted to expose Fred to something. I don't believe Fred got the best of it though. Some years later at a class reunion, I recalled this with Fred and we had an extended visit. Fred was with the Coast Guard and was in charge of surveillance on the Gulf Atlantic Coasts. I asked him what the biggest problem was. He said the exporting of blue-eyed blondes, preferably 115 pounds. I asked why he couldn't control it. He said they were all brainwashed when they decided to go overseas for lucrative promises. Most of them then disappeared. Hitler in Mein Kampf loathed this.

—B.C. Ahouse

#52 – Wednesday November 22, 2000

My good friend Stanley A. had seven sisters, who always kept him pressed and ironed. We were both good in school. In fact, one time our physics teacher in our senior year told us there wasn't anymore we could learn since we had read the book. Just behave in class. When Stanley was called up for the Army in 1941, we had a party in the woods. We were roasting hot dogs on a stick over an open fire. I accidentally poked Stanley in the eye, which made it a red mess. However, he wrote me from Puerto Rico, sending a photo of him lounging on a beach chair. His damaged eye, he said, was a blessing in disguise. We are still friends. He always said he considered both him and I lucky.

— B.C. Ahouse

#53 – Wednesday November 22, 2000

I started school in Wilkes Barre after turning six years old the previous April—that was the rule. I walked over half a mile to Hayt Street School, passing a pretzel bakery on the way where you could get two large pretzels for a penny if you had one. I believe my teacher was a Miss Guffy. One oddity I recall is us boys always eager to watch a boy urinate simply because his penis had two heads. There was a man who sold candy on the sidewalk for a penny each. I remember candy watermelons were prevalent. In my class were two girl twins; they asked for some candy but didn't have any pennies. The man gave them some for the ring each wore on their fingers. Their mother was furious and called the candy man the next day. He became violent, pulled out a knife and cut off his ear. I recall gathering around it as it lay on the ground. Police came after him and the man ran away.

— B.C. Ahouse

#54 – Wednesday November 22, 2000

In April 1922, because my father lost his house on Barney Street in Wilkes Barre, we moved to Washington Street in Nanticoke, PA I went to the nearby Washington Street School. Miss Pratt (a friend of our family) was the first grade teacher. The first test in spelling was for 25 words. I missed one. I spelled scene as seen and was marked wrong. The teacher told me to come up and hold out my right hand; I thought it was for a reward. I did, and she cracked it with a wooden paddle. Then also the left hand. I couldn't believe it. I cried. It was at this time that I quit smoking. Most of the boys had a small Uncle Sam Pipe in which they smoked discarded cigarette butts. I just joined the gang (the last time I did any). One day my mother, Edith, found my pipe, lectured me on it, and then whaled the lights out of me. Except for an occasional cigar at Christenings, I never had a desire to smoke, and I am probably the youngest person to permanently quit smoking.

—B.C. Ahouse

#55 – Wednesday November 22, 2000

This was started many years ago and is entirely by
me.

Throughout man's years-long history
He's oft dwelt on the word "shit"
It's true meaning was usually quite murky
This poem should clarify it

Bullshit is a byproduct
From the making of most cheese
Tis also a quaint expression
Of one's trying to displease.

Horseshit comes in a neater package
As most of us should know
Like the oily words of a salesman
When he's really trying to show.

Chicken shit is a gagging matter
By the Army made renown
Where a smile is easily killed
By a Non-Com's ugly frown.

Ape shit is a romantic notion
That pushes many a man along
Who thinks he's a swinging hero
But is usually a foolish clown.

Tough shit is a hardening period
When we all feel utmost distress.
It was bad enough in days gone by
But much worse since high interest.

No shit is a sidestepping motion
When there is nothing else we can say
It would be nicer to be agreeable
But whoever was born that way?

If after reading this composition
You feel slightly like a fool
Put your thoughts at ease and know
That all shit can be used as a tool.

— Bernard C. Ahouse

#56 – Thanksgiving Thursday – November 23, 2000

Another of John's stories or jokes. His father was a Banker in Sommerville Tennessee and often told of the stranger who came in and requested a loan of $1500.00. The client was asked his name, which he said was Joe Blow. He was also asked what he needed the money for. Joe said he wanted to put a much-needed bathroom in his house. After asking about his means and method of repayment, the banker asked where he had been doing his business. In desperation Joe replied, "Out in the bushes." That's why he needed the bathroom.

—B.C. Ahouse

#57 – Thanksgiving Thursday – November 23, 2000

Six years ago this Thanksgiving, I left Irene, reluctantly, in the Geneva General Hospital. I said reluctantly because of the fiasco in the Emergency Room. Also all tests showed her negative—Dr. B replaced Dr. LaG and foolishly administered H to Irene to prevent a stroke—simply because Irene asked him if she had one. Susan was observant, as her attached letter shows. I agree with her. Her opinion of Dr. Alain, I believe, is correct. I enter this because of Dr. M. Lindermouth asking me to sign a complaint against Dr. Alain—Robert Herrick was present.

—B.C. Ahouse

4/7/97
Mr. Bernard Ahouse
R.D. Smith Road
Lodi, New York 46381

Dear Dad,

As you requested, I am writing this re-cap of what I observed the night Mom was taken into surgery at the Geneva hospital in November 1994.

When I arrived from D.C., she was resting in bed in a standard room. We had a short conversation (you were present), but she was very tired and we did not stay long. It seemed no sooner had we gotten home, we were called back to the hospital, as Mom was being taken into intensive care.

We arrived and they would only allow one of us in at a time, so I waited while you went to see her. After you came out, I went in, and I was shocked at how pale she was. She was trying to be cheerful and didn't want me to worry, but she was so afraid. You and I waited together for some time. As it got later and later with no announced change, I encouraged you to go home to get some much-needed sleep. My daughters showed up and were there to be with me, so you eventually did leave.

As the night passed (I recall it was very late but cannot tell you the hour, one a.m. maybe), I came and went from Mom's bed many times, as did Lisa, Laura and Emily in turn. What I saw in that room scared me more than I ever have been in my life. Mom was hemorrhaging so profusely that the nurse was holding a bedpan to catch the flow, as pads were nowhere near enough to collect the blood. I believe they told me that they had transfused eight pints of blood at that point, but she was bleeding faster than they could replace it.

Finally, a Dr. Alain arrived and I was informed that he was the surgeon that was going to operate. It seemed forever before they took Mom to the operating room, during which time I called you to let you know what was going on. I asked what was taking so long and was told that they were trying to build her blood volume so that they could operate. Dr. Alain and I spoke briefly, and I learned that he was not the doctor that had been attending Mom but was called in to perform the surgery.

He explained that "build up her blood volume" really meant that they were giving blood under pressure to attempt to overcome her loss. He had little other information to give me, but as they took her to OR, he told me that it did not look good at all and that he gave her a 50/50 chance of survival. He promised me he would do the best he could... but she had already lost so much blood!

I, personally, have no doubt in my mind that Dr. Alain saved Mom's life. Whatever went on before or after, I know that if that man had not operated when he did, she would not be with us today. I am so adamant in my belief that I would gladly do whatever necessary to support Dr. Alain.

I know how helpless we all felt through Mom's ordeal and how very happy we all were that she survived, but still, it's awful to think that with all the technology we have today, Mom's condition was left to deteriorate to the state she was when taken to surgery. Wherever the fault lies, it most certainly is not with Dr. Alain.

My very best to you and Mom. I'll speak to you soon.

Much love,

Susan Ahouse

1545 No. Colonial Terrace

#101

Arlington, VA 22209

#58 – Thanksgiving Thursday – November 23, 2000

About the time I got out of high school in Nanticoke, PA, Dr. Barney Steguso started his practice. I recall my father Bernard, he carbon-penciled his portrait. I used to drive Dr. Steguso around on his house visits. One memorable time he came out laughing saying the daughter had just given birth to a Coca-Cola Bottle (a douche). Barney had a brother, Stanley, who he set up next door to his elaborate office as a funeral director. This parlor next to the doctor drew questions and laughter. However, an advertisement from December 30, 1997 tops anything I ever saw before. The Geneva General Hospital own their own funeral home — The Devanery Bennett Funeral Home, right handy to the hospital.

— B.C. Ahouse

#59 – Thanksgiving Thursday – November 23, 2000

Anthony F. Izbicki and I have been close friends since 1927. We were together the night he met his future and present wife, Ms. Mickie Cherry of Len Lyoula. Their first child, Tony Jr., was born while my friend was in the Marine Corps in 1943. Young Tony went through college and started a company called Hood Metals—since bought by a French company who retained Tony to manage it. Tony Jr. had a son, Kevin, who I have known since his birth. He was a good student and went through law school. A newspaper article explains his horrible mistake. After the murder, he dismembered his mother's body, leaving it in trunk, which on its discovery led to his apprehension at Princeton University.

—B.C. Ahouse

#60 – Thanksgiving Thursday, November 23, 2000

During the early months of 1943, I was in the Station Hospital in Fort Belvoir, Virginia recuperating from pneumonia. One evening, a Jewish captain, a doctor, told the young fellow in the bed next to me to turn on his side so he could examine him. He started to do a rectal finger exam but didn't stop even though the boy began screaming. I got up, put my hand on his shoulder, and said, "Stop it, Captain."

He said, "Do you know what you are doing?"

I said, "Yes. And, also what you're doing."

Shortly after this, two interns told me to get up and follow them. I spent the night in the Death Room with two men who died that night of spinal meningitis. I thank God I didn't catch it. Nothing more came out of this incident.

—B.C. Ahouse

#61 – Friday November 24, 2000

I lived in Binghamton, New York during the middle of the 1940s. The congressman was Edwin Arthur Hall. He was known as the constituents' friend; willing to answer any question or take on any task. The one memorable to me was his being asked why the hamlet of Chenango Forks, New York had a much higher birthrate than the rest of Broome County. He and his aides came up with the explanation that at 5:00 a.m. two freight trains passed through the village, and by law loudly sounded their whistles at several crossings. Naturally, it woke almost everybody up. Obviously, it was too early to get up and too late or hard to get back to sleep. Naturally, couples took good use of the interlude; hence, an enhanced birthrate.

—B.C. Ahouse

#62 – Friday November 24, 2000

While at Fort Belvoir, Virginia in 1942-1943, I made the acquaintance of three men. Morris Greentree of Richmond, Va., Fernando J Palicio of Havana, Cuba, and Sam S., an artist from Wilkes Barre, PA. They were quite friendly with me, and although I was welcome in their company, I couldn't afford it financially. I left the Army earlier than they, but kept some contact. I was married and my first-born son, Karl, was an individual to himself. Perhaps he was unduly influenced by his friend Neil Kerns. With Neil's help, Karl, to put it bluntly, ran away by Greyhound bus, taking a shotgun and 270 Winchester Rifle with him. I just knew this phone call was coming from the police in Richmond, Va telling me the boy was in serious trouble. In desperation, I called Morris Greentree, whose family had some influence there and explained the situation, asking if he could help. A day or so later, Karl was back home with his guns. Morris never commented.

—B.C. Ahouse

#63 – Friday November 24, 2000

Some 40 years ago, I did quite a bit of plumbing and heating work to keep the farm going. I put in the plumbing and hot air heating for two schoolteachers, both their wives being schoolteachers too. Jim VanGalio got the normal installation, but Si Meyers wanted two johns, side-by-side, which I did. Without my knowledge, they removed some of the fixtures to install some wall covering but weren't able to reset them. They asked me to do so, which I agreed to after I completed plumbing work at Dr. Brownell's, a dentist in Ovid, New York. This wasn't good enough for them and the two couples (four people) showed up at the doctor's office chanting, "Bernie Ahouse is unfair!" They kept this up for a good 15 minutes. Eventually, I reinstalled their fixtures.

—B.C. Ahouse

#64 – Friday November 24, 2000

Shortly after the war in the late forties, early fifties, two brothers on occasion worked with us on the farm. Bob and Jim Ferguson were as fine and well kept as any who did so. Both went into the Army or Air Force and became pilots, on occasion buzzing the farm for sport. I believe it was Bob who had to parachute in to Hanford, Oregon Atomic Base and was held there for an unreasonable time. About 25 years ago, I heard the news on the car radio and could hardly believe that Jim and his son had drowned in Cayuga (or Seneca) Lake while moving a boatload of cement to their cottage site. He was just too intelligent to have done this. Both had become pilots for Mohawk Airlines and flew over the farm. I mentioned that they seemed low in bad weather. Bob said it was because they stayed at two thousand feet, which was still above our altitude.

— B.C. Ahouse

#65 – Friday November 24, 2000

At Cornell University, Ithaca

About 50 years ago, I had brief contact with Professors Watson and Make regarding a jet engine obtained from Nazi Germany. My bit of information didn't amount to much, but when I heard while in Stuart, Florida that the Saturn Rocket was going to be tested at the Pratt and Whitney installation, I decided I'd like to see it. I got into the base by applying for a job. The personnel officer questioned me about my experience and I listed the machines and authority I had at the Westover, NY Hamilton Plant. He asked me when. I said about ten years ago. He sarcastically asked me if I could still do it. I said, yes. He then asked me what else I thought I could do. I said, "Let me get on that side of the table and I'll show you how to do your job. He called security, after checking me out, and I got the pass for the test. The engine shattered a layer of black concrete it was bolted to.

— B.C. Ahouse

#66 – Friday November 24, 2000

About 1980, while in the Florida Keys, I was recuperating from an unnecessary kidney stone operation and doing some fishing. The place I bought shrimp bait had two old guys playing checkers before a sign saying, "Free Advice". After a while, I asked them for some of their free advice. One pointed a finger at me and said, "Never add water to whiskey." They did at the factory. During this period of time, I used to fish off a well-traveled bridge between Duck Key and Marathon. The traffic was always a concern. The sidewalk was quite narrow. There was a guard railing above the water. The last time I fished there, I had just moved away from the traffic to toss my line in when a pickup truck with extended foot-square mirrors that had not been folded in barely missed my head. I felt the breeze. The truck was going at a high speed. This was one of many close calls I had over the years.

—B.C. Ahouse

#67 – Friday November 24, 2000

About two years ago, while in Atlantic City's Resort Casino, an older fellow came over and asked who I was. I said Bernie Ahouse. He said he was Al S who formerly ran ST's chicken hatchery, and who I years ago bought baby chicks from (Red Rocks). We got reacquainted and he told me that he made good earnings playing black jack. He had to go to court to be allowed to play in New Jersey casinos. He prevailed and suggested I consider it. I never gave it a try. Also, he acquainted me with his nephew, Mack Ste of New York City and Los Angeles, a high-ranked banker.

— B.C. Ahouse

#68 – Friday November 24, 2000

About 1980, when I was recuperating in the Florida Keys, I often went fishing from an old bridge on Big Pine Key. I had frequented the same place several days in a row when a fellow came up, got quite close, and threw a line in. He nudged me once too often and I asked him if he would like me to throw him in the water. He told me he was John Phelps of the U.S. Coast Guard, down from Oswego, New York. I identified myself and my credentials. He made some apology and mentioned a bail of Marijuana behind some bushes a short piece away and supposed I knew of it. I said, "No, what's the deal?" He said there was 30 pounds of cocaine in the bale. After the amenities, he suggested that I partake in the sale of seized cars and boats… I declined.

— B.C. Ahouse

#69 – Saturday November 25, 2000

The first I heard of Mel Fisher, the treasure hunter, was when a huge trove of gold coins that I believe he retrieved of Ft. Pierce, Florida was exhibited in the lobby of a bank in Lake Worth, Florida. They were arranged in an open pile on a large round table in full access to the public. My wife Irene and I made the visit to see such a treasure. Irene struck up a conversation with the loan guard who oversaw the display. She asked him if she could pick up a coin. He said it would be OK for her to do so. At the moment she picked up a gold piece, a schoolteacher with a bunch of small children came in. On seeing what Irene did, they gathered around and did likewise. The guard paled, but I believe all the coins were returned.

—B.C. Ahouse

#70 – Saturday November 25, 2000

About 1980, while staying in Marathon, Florida, I became aware of a court hearing to be held in Big Pine Key shortly regarding the State of Florida's claim to the treasure ship *Atocha* as an archaeological site. I listened to the state's excuses and motions. I also noticed that several men who made a business of running glass-bottomed boats over exhausted sites were gleefully touching Mr. Fisher. I addressed the judge, saying I was a friend of the court and may I speak. I told him I was an ancient conservationist and presently visiting Florida. I also had been a member of the NYS Conservation District State Board. He consented. I briefly and forcefully stated that Mel Fisher had paid dearly in developing this site and that it should be his; that if the state wanted likewise, they should find it for themselves.

–B.C. Ahouse

#71 – Saturday November 25. 2000

Mel Fisher's office was a replica of, I believe, the *Santa Maria*. It leaked and he had placed a canvas around the outside of the hull from which he pumped the water out to keep it afloat. After the court hearing in Big Pine Key, Irene and I visited him on the boat. He thanked me for my support and said that if I could make the $10,000 investment, he would give me $10,000 of emeralds up front. With the farm situation as it was I just didn't have the money. When we came on board, several police officers were leaving. Since it was rumored that Mel had been arrested for gold smuggling, I asked if that was what it was about. He said no, a silver block the size of a box of bread had been stolen. I asked if he thought it could be recovered. He said he didn't care. He knew who took it, and he needed it more than him. He then mentioned the gold chain that he was wrongly accused of smuggling and that he had just retrieved it. He got it out and draped it around Irene's neck. It must have been 15 feet long. I said to Irene, "Run! He won't chase you for it." She didn't, but it was quite an experience.

—B.C. Ahouse

#72 – Saturday November 25, 2000

I have never been impressed by people saluting each other or by them emphasizing their self-importance. Over the years, I have coined an expression that usually deflates an ego. I quote it as thus: "You seem to allude to a pretension of intelligence and authority, which I fail to detect. Would you care to elaborate on it?" I don't mean this as an insult, merely an honest suggestion to take a second look at oneself. In every respect, there is usually a muted change in attitude and contact.

— B.C. Ahouse

#73 – Saturday November 25, 2000

Twenty or so years ago, my son-in-law Don gave me a Steuben Glass Co Bi-Centennial eagle as a Christmas gift. However, it was not signed. We admired it by putting it on display on a coffee table in our living room. As children at times are tempted or curious, my grandson Joseph picked it up and ran out to our kitchen to show it to his mother, who shouted at him for doing so. He dropped it and chipped it, but luckily on the bottom, not the head. I prevailed upon an acquaintance to have it repaired, which he had done at Stueben Glass in Corning. It came back signed "Steuben." Later, my son-in-law happened to pick it up. His eyes almost popped out when he saw the signature. I never explained it to him.

— B.C. Ahouse

#74 – Sunday November 26, 2000

Sometime in the mid 1920s, I and my friend Bernard Wasilewski were with our parents vacationing at Lake, PA. One morning we wandered down to the lake, where a fisherman towed a boat which had been adrift to a dock. We got in it and paddled around. Tired of it, when we got out the boat got away and was again adrift. We decided to walk over to his relatives' farm a mile or so away where we spent the day. On our return to the lake, we went down to where a large crowd had gathered. Someone had told our parents they earlier saw us in the boat. Someone finally recognized us and called our parents, who after their joy or relief, soundly spanked us for going off so. The climax to this story is that we both wrote it as an essay for our English class in high school. Our teacher tore both copies up saying one of us must have copied.

— B.C. Ahouse

#75 – Sunday November 26, 2000

While we were in our teens, my good friend Anthony (Budgie) Izbicki and I hitchhiked to Lake Selk Worth from our homes in Nanticoke. We spent some time with friends and swimming. In mid-afternoon, we started for home and were picked up by a storeowner named I believe Nalbach. He was driving a four-door Model H Sedan. The passenger seat in front and the middle of the backseat were stacked with wooden crates of empty glass bottles. Going downhill right above where the road entered from Dalles, his brakes failed and he hit a flatbed hauling a large piece of equipment. The engine of the car came through the dash and into the backseat. We weren't badly hurt, but I believe the man was killed. Budgie took off running (he was scared). I followed him. No one ever looked us up.

— B.C. Ahouse

#76 – Sunday November 26, 2000

In 1975, while at the National Conservation District Convention in Denver, I got to know some reps from Coors Brewery in Golden, Colorado. They invited us to take a tour of their facility. I was most interested in the malting tank. I was. It was over a thousand feet long. The longer it took for the barley to move through it, the darker the beer. We were given a private tour by our acquaintance, who was quite talkative. He told us that Coors had taken every bit of information it could get about beer, entered it in a computer and then asked for the simplest narrative about beer. The answer was, "You never buy it. You just rent it."

– B.C. Ahouse

#77 – Sunday November 26, 2000

Because of my observations while traveling, I suggested to the N.Y.S. Conservation District Board that we should suggest and support a deposit law on bottles and cans. Most all agreed, and we had the secretary draw up a motion which was forwarded to the assembly. They declined and told us to forget it. After some discussion, I suggested to Howard Findly (who besides being our chairman, also chaired the Cayuga County Board of Supervisors) that he present it to his board. They approved it and made it law in Cayuga County. Since the industry was stuck with this, it eventually became the law of New York State. It sure helped clean up the highways. What happened to the unclaimed millions?

—B.C. Ahouse

#78 – Sunday November 26, 2000

I assisted Ms. Alice Larsen in formulating a letter and submitted it for record.

— B.C Ahouse

#79 – Monday November 27, 2000

I stepped out the back door of my office about six years ago right on top of a large raccoon. The animal grabbed my left shoe. I stepped on his head and ran around to pound on a window to alert my wife Irene not to follow—she thought I had lost my marbles. Anyhow, she did open another door. I came in and loaded a twelve-gauge double-barreled shotgun—two shells was a grave mistake. I did know that a .22 caliber never stopped a rabid animal. I cracked open the door. The raccoon tried to get in, so I pulled the trigger and killed him. Somehow, I dropped the gun. Luckily, it was not aimed at me when it went off. I got some of the fluids on my hand from the animal. I called Charles Carrol, the health officer, asking if I should get shots for rabies. He said under the circumstances I'd have to pay $24,000 for them. Recalling all the times I risked my life for dollars a day, I decided no. I filled the bathtub with a gallon of Clorox and water and soaked. All is OK.

— B.C. Ahouse

#80 – Monday November 27, 2000

One day in the 1970s, I began to combine wheat with my International 401 Machine. At that time, there was no cab on it. I was in the field on the NE Corner of Dean + CR 137, and was making the second round of the field going north on the east side. I was approaching a steep drop-off towards Mill Creek, but although the ground was rain soft, I was almost 20 feet from the edge and felt safe. Although the rain was falling, without warning the combine began to slide toward the right and suddenly completely overturned. I took the best chance as I saw it and slid between the seat and grain bin. With the combine completely upside down, it slid down the incline about a hundred feet. The wheat was scattered, but only my pride was hurt. Karl and cleaned up the wheat. Ronnie Swich, a body man, mostly repaired the damage to the Auger.

– B.C. Ahouse

#81 – Monday November 27, 2000

In the early 1970s, we were attending my first National Conservation Convention in Washington, D.C. We were at the hotel near which President Regan was later shot. It was here that I met Bud Tucker and Fred Cormack. Hagg Boggs also made an appearance, which was shortly before the flight he took during which he disappeared. The ladies at the office were invited to a tea in the White House, which was hosted by Julie Eisenhower since her parents Richard and Mrs. Nixon were leaving on a trip to China. "Her first," Irene met Julie and enjoyed the circumstances. There was a musical event going on and Irene asked a guard who the group was since they were not identified. He briskly said, "Madame, that is the U.S. Marine Corps Band."

—B.C. Ahouse

#82 – Monday November 27, 2000

About 1980, Philip Thornton, the head of the Forest Service in D.C., called me and asked if I would come to address the meeting at the Eisenhower College Campus regarding the Cayuga Indian claim he had first made me aware of. I said no thanks. Later he called Irene and asked her if she would, and she said yes. At the college, the disrupted night Irene gave a speech expressing her views on the matter, the crowd started to boo her, shouting insults. Irene, after it quieted down, simply said, "I'd sooner have red skins for my neighbors than red necks." It was on the front page of the *Rochester Democrat Chronicle* the next day.

John Townsend soon called, demanding to know why I had Irene speak so. I said, "You may tell your wife what to say John, but I don't."

– B.C. Ahouse

#83 – Monday November 27, 2000

While assigned to Mitchell Field, New York in 1942 by the United Stated Engineers Department of 120 Wall St White Hall Bldg, I was assigned to the inspection of a guardhouse being built at the north entrance opposite Roosevelt Field Airport. The plans for the building looked sound to me, but for the fact that it was being constructed as a concrete roadway with the joint of the road seemingly in the center of the building. I called this to the attention of M. Molitor, my supervisor. But also put it in my written notes. The building was built and on the first freeze the road constricted and the guardhouse, being built of glass blocks, split in two. M. Molitor took a view of my mention and my warning.

—B.C. Ahouse

#84 – Monday November 27, 2000

While at Mitchell Field in 1942, I witnessed two accidents. The first involved a British Lancaster Bomber that had just come in from England. It taxied up to a hangar, and while its huge propellers were still slowly turning, a dump truck backed out of a hangar into the propeller, which didn't show too much damage to me. However, it sliced the steel truck body up like bread.

The second involved a USA B26 bomber. I was talking to some of the 20 or so men in it before they were to take off for England (I believe). The plane taxied down to the far airstrip apron. When the pilot revved up the engines, a propeller broke off and flew high in the air. I saw one man get to the top before it exploded in flames. All were lost.

– B.C. Ahouse

#85 – Monday November 27, 2000

In 1938 or 1939, my Aunt Olga's husband hired me to deepen his well in red shale in the village of Nuaugola, where he had built a fine house but had no water. Fred MacLaughlin Sr. had dug the well to about 30 feet and William S., Aunt Olga's husband, wanted it 20 feet deeper. I got Stanley Rosencrans, a friend and neighbor, to work with me. He held the jumper while I hammered it. I packed the dynamite and electric blasting caps. Stanley worked the wrench and five-gallon bucket to haul up the tailings. We did this while the Suntkens went to the world fair in NYC, and after they got back, we got a little water, but not much. The Suntkens' son Hubert had a dog "Dandy", and since he usually got his way, we lowered Dandy down to the bottom of the well (about 50 feet). Going down didn't bother the dog, but coming up did. He started yelping and barking and when the bucket came by the horizontal pipe from the cellar, Dandy wrapped his four legs around it. When Hubert cranked the bucket out from in under the dog, he (the dog) held on to the pipe for a while but then plunged to the bottom. The water probably cushioned his fall. Stanley went down, put the dog in the bucket, covered it with a bag, and Dandy returned to the surface. Probably the only dog in the world that ever enjoyed such an adventure.

— B.C Ahouse

#85B – Tuesday November 28, 2000

My first encounter with a Holstein bull occurred when I was a young boy. I was on what we called Kelly's Field (in Nanticoke, PA) when a large bull came running toward me. I jumped into a nearby mine cove. I had a hard time getting out. The next occurred on our farm in Lodi, NY, where we still live. I let a bull out of his pen, and he immediately turned on me. I ran to get over a wall. He barely missed me with his charge, imbedding a horn in a wall. I ran to the house, got a rifle, and shot the critter. I immediately butchered him, not knowing not to kill an enraged animal if you intended to eat him. I learned later that the meal was bound to be tough. My wife prepared it for lunch for our crew — including a planter working here. Irene said, "Tough huh? Louie Smith said it'd probably be tougher if we didn't have meat."

— B.C. Ahouse

#86 – Tuesday November 28, 2000

About 1950, I had Charles Far dig a drainage ditch on the east side of mill creek. His floating chain excavator left the bottom uneven, and I manually leveled it out. One afternoon as I stood up, a bull — steer — which I didn't notice almost hooked me with his horn. I dropped down in the ditch, crawled to the creek embankment and ran home. I called the owner, Lee Skinner, telling him I wouldn't shoot the animal if he got him off my land first. He did and called me the next morning to come over, since he and neighbor Don Johnson were going to butcher him. The bull was in a solid enclosed pen, east of Lee's home. He gave Don a single shot .22 rife and Don entered the pen. Lee shut the door. Don missed with the first shot and the bull went wild. Don screamed and pounded on the door. Lee opened it slightly and handed Don another bullet. Luckily, that one worked. The animal was a poorly pushed castrated steer.

— B.C Ahouse

#87 – Monday November 28, 2000

After reminiscing about Lee Skinner, I have to mention the time he brought an A.C. combine here for some welding. My young son Karl, out of curiosity, stuck his finger in a hole on the combine. It immediately swelled up, and he couldn't pull it out. Lee, who was trimming some hay from a shaft, had a knife in his hand. He came over to Karl and said, "I'll get you loose." Karl yelled, fearing the knife. Lee pinched the finger and the swelling left. Karl ran away.

Another time, I was to help Lee plane some lumber for the barn we were building. His man, Roger Letter, in moving a tractor to put a belt on the Pla, backed into the pulley shaft and bent it. Lee said he'd fix it. He had the belt put on the pulley and thought he could straighten it out by running it slowly. It started to do so, and he revved up the speed. The vibration shattered the heavy cushion frame. A piece about the size of a wedge used for splitting wood broke loose. It hit a wooden part about one foot from my face. I couldn't pull it loose.

– B.C. Ahouse

#88 – Tuesday November 28, 2000

My niece Jennifer's husband introduced me to Leo Murphy, an attorney from Olean, NY. Leo first represented me in Ithaca, NY regarding an interest rate problem I had with the Tompkins Co. Trust Company. After hearing the problem, the judge said plainly, "You aren't going to make me famous — settle this on the sidewalk." My friend Robert Herred thanked me for teaching him a lesson. On another occasion, they tried to foreclose three houses after their computer showed me in default. In Rochester, the judge denied the motion saying he'd sooner believe Bernard Ahouse than the bank. Leo approached the matter in a fashion he chose, and we ended up in Corning. Judge Purple said I should accept the bank's offer of $10,000 to me, and my deeding the property to the bank. I disagreed and said after his insistence, "Where is that written in the Constitution?"

He said, "Don't smart ass me... take it."

I said to Leo, "If I do, I wouldn't pay you a cent."

He said OK.

When I delivered the deeds to the bank attorney in Rochester, they said they would send the check after they recorded the deeds. I said good and started out. They came up with the check.

—B.C. Ahouse

#89 – Tuesday November 28, 2000

In 1974, I believe we were in Houston, Texas for the NACD Convention. We went to see the shows. Sonny and Cher were there, but Cher wouldn't come out of the trailer in the arena. One evening I was at a dinner meeting including Earl Butz (Nixon's Secretary of Agriculture) and Bob of Waco, Texas, chairman of the Agricultural Committee. Earl Butz rambled on about how important we farmers were to the world economy and well-being. He said the world would need all the grain that we could produce and that we would be well paid for it. Later, when I got in an elevator, Bob P was already in it. He invited me up to his room to help him with a bottle of bourbon. I did. Reflecting on Earl Butz's remarks, he simply said to me, "Don't believe that Republican SOB." Shortly after Butz told a colored joke that finished him.

— B.C. Ahouse

#90 – Tuesday November 28, 2000

In 1973-74, I built and later sold a house on the Segar Lot in Horseheads, New York. A Gordon Herbert, who came here from Michigan to head the National Homes Plant in Horseheads, bought it. He moved in before the closing and found everything fine. I had mortgaged the property with the Marine Midland Bank in Elmira. At the closing, Elmira Savings financed the purchase to G. Herbert. My attorney, Everet Wayermilla had the mortgage, which I examined, and he was to record. Instead of the Elmira Savings Bank paying M.M. the $25,000, they gave it to Gordon Herbert, who then found everything possible wrong with the house. M.M. demanded that I give them the 25 grand. I said the discharge would prove that they were paid. I could not locate it in the courthouse. Later, Dan Tush, a P.I., found it under "D", where it should have been filed. He posed as a janitor, I believe.

— B.C. Ahouse

#91 – Wednesday November 29, 2000

Following the discovery of the discharge of mortgage by Dan Tusch, Everet W. would not represent me. I finally got George Welch of Corning to take the matter against Elmira Savings. After much wrangling, Judge S Wood ruled in my favor. Elmira Savings appealed, and it went to the court in Albany, New York. The judges there refused to reverse the verdict and somehow the whole matter got set aside and settled. I may add that George W. was reluctant to handle this and only did after Paul Molson of NYC, an attorney, threatened him if he didn't. The complete record is in my files.

– B.C. Ahouse

#92 – Wednesday November 29, 2000

While I was chairing the Seneca County Conservation District Board, a man, Angelo Tantello, appeared before it and asked for permission to create a landfill business in Seneca County. His idea was to remove the topsoil, fill in six to eight feet of garbage, restore the topsoil and thereby increase the drainage and production of food to feed the needy people of the world. The board agreed, so I signed his permit. The landfill business took off and Tantello sold out to a Rochester firm now called Seneca Meadows. There has been much controversy about it all, and the fill has now grown into a sizable mountain. The company is asking to increase the size again. Seneca Falls receives a considerable amount of money for this.

—B.C. Ahouse

#93 – Wednesday November 29, 2000

Time for another joke. Phily Thornton the head of the Forest Service related this to us in Houston. On the flight down from Washington, D.C., he said he had the pleasure to be seated next to an attractive and sociable lady, Mrs. Kirby, which made the flight a pleasure. As the dialogue became friendlier, he commented about the large diamond ring she was sporting. She said, "Oh yes, it is known as one of the best ever found." Phil asked if it had any notoriety such as the Hope Diamond.

She said, "In what way?"

He said, "Is there any curse attached to it?"

She said, "Of Course. Mr. Kirby."

— B.C. Ahouse

#94 – Wednesday November 29, 2000

While at Fort Dix, New Jersey in August 1942, we were housed in square-peaked tents. I was held there for quite a spell waiting to be shipped out. This was a receiving center. We enjoyed the supervisor, a little corporal who couldn't properly handle what little authority he had. He somehow got into quite a situation with a fellow from Brooklyn, I think named G. It led to the corporal calling our captain to reprimand him. The captain stood outside the tent and shouted something like, "If there is a man there by the name of G., will he step out?" G. did so, thinking the captain wanted to fight. He cold-cocked him and ended up in Ft. Leavenworth, Kansas for the war, later becoming famous, as Rocky.

– B.C. Ahouse

#95 – Wednesday November 29, 2000

Early in 1997, I visited the Geneva General Hospital by appointment. A Mr. Robert Herrick accompanied me. We met with a Dr. Marten Linderworth, who asked what he could do for me. I said to correct the prognosis of my wife Irene's admittance in November 1994 and wipe out the tail ends of many bills outstanding. He said no. But then he asked me to sign a complaint against a Dr. Dan Alain; a surgeon who I believe saved Irene's life after the hospital fouled up. I said I couldn't do that, but the matter was directed to the NYS Health Department, which condemned the hospital. I later called Dr. Linderworth asking if I could talk to him again. He simply said, "Get a lawyer to talk to me." I did.

– B.C. Ahouse

#96 – Wednesday November 29, 2000

After refusal from Shapiro-Bell and Irene's refusal to deal with John Nicet, someone referred me to Joanne Hunt P. She provided a new rate to me (a basic 30%) and I provided her with a retainer. And I sent additional funds as needed. She did a fine job through the first two years of litigation. My one complaint as I told her was her not telling me of her new position and her involving J.H. without my knowledge. And also, an agreement not telling me of the judge being replaced by Patricia Marks Harrell misled us into B. Insurance Company's offer and their making it a blanket for all defendants. I reluctantly signed after Irene did. The judge got us to do so. There is a gag order on us in this matter.

— B.C. Ahouse

#97 – Nipped in the Bud

There is a story by Bernard Ahouse of 61 W. Washington Street, Nanticoke, PA.

#98 – Thursday November 30, 2000

Dear Viola and Graham

To occupy myself I have begun to write my memoirs. Not to be a narrative as such, just a collection of events that I witnessed and experienced. My memory seems to be in excellent shape, so before it fails altogether, I will continue to set them down. In going through some papers, I found your letter of 24 January 1998. I've been a long time in replying. You mentioned Viola's arthritic knees. I too developed severe pain in my left knee. The V.A. has supplied me with a Capsaicn 0.025%. Perhaps it may aid Viola as it does me.

Good luck,

Bernie C. Ahouse

#99 – Thursday November 30, 2000

Up until December 1995, I experienced the theft of various objects and material from the shop and storage area on our farm. Although my agent, Phil I., supported my claim for losses, the insurance company's adjuster, a Ken Bohrman of Geneva Adjustment, would not pay. He submitted the enclosed non-waiver agreement form which two attorneys, Stuart Miller and David B, could not understand and told me not to sign it. The BCI investigator, a woman after her husband retired, was of no help and practically ignored the thefts.

—B.C. Ahouse

#100 – Thursday November 30, 2000

About 30 years ago, I bought several farms from Roger Love in Hector, New York—Schuyler County. Included was a drawer-type John Deere combine. In the process of cleaning it up, I found a Zippo lighter under the cylinder in the concave. It was completely flattened—about the size of a silver dollar. Many years later, I was having dinner at the Oil Producers Club in Bradford, PA with a group of associates. A person came by and was asked to join us. He was introduced as the CEO of Zippo Lighter Co. I asked if they still guaranteed the lighters. He said, "Unconditionally."

I said I had a dandy.

He said, "Send it to me." I did. He had it straightened out, new inserts put in, and he returned it to me. The case shows the effects of being flattened. I still have it.

—B.C. Ahouse

#101 – Thursday November 30, 2000

The present fiasco in the presidential election in Florida brings to mind the first time I voted for a president, in 1940. Wendel Wilkie was my choice over FDR when I entered the mechanical voting booth. I couldn't lock the mechanism. The watchers immediately asked what I did. I didn't do anything. The person prior to me was the priest from St. Mary's Church, a Father Lewindowski. He came over and said let the boy go. Apparently someone had dropped something behind the levers and jammed the machine. This also reminds me of the father's foster son, Anthony, who I was told by his friend that he was the one who had stolen all of my rabbits. Perhaps he did.

– B.C. Ahouse

#102 – Thursday November 30, 2000

Don't misunderstand my interest in this matter. If one Jew or Gypsy was killed in the manner described by the Holocaust, it was wrong. I first had doubts of the situation when pictures of hundreds of corpses stacked like cordwood were exhibited. For what purpose could this be done? During the war, the RAF bombed the Rhine River dorms, drowning thousands. Does this explain the absurd photos? Also, the Soviet archives recently released should shed some light on the subject. Recently, columnist Carl Kraut Hammer chastised fellow Jews for capitalizing unduly for profit.

— B.C. Ahouse

#103 – Thursday November 30, 2000

On this day 25 years ago, our dear friend Adelaide Gleisner was to be buried. I was combining oats on the Neal farm. I wasn't in the best frame of mind and when the auger on the 401.1HC combine plugged, I disconnected the drive and climbed up on the drive wheel not realizing that the cylinder was still revolving. I tugged on the drive belt on the auger, carelessly leaving my middle left finger being dragged around the pulley by the belt. My finger was completely turned 180 degrees out of place. I immediately turned it back in place. It exploded like a balloon. At the funeral parlor, several said I should see a doctor. No one was going to touch it. Today it is about normal.

– B.C. Ahouse

#104 – Friday December 1, 2000

When I was in my middle teens, I often walked to my grandmother's (Lena Burman's) farm, basically because there was always plenty to eat. That is probably why I decided young in life to someday become a farmer and own a farm. There was also the added attraction of hunting, which my uncles thoroughly enjoyed. (Particularly Uncle Charles Brush) My step-grandfather, "Pop" Leopold Burman, had an old single-barreled twelve-gauge shotgun, which he frequently let me use. One time when I fired it, the breach (tinged barrel) flared out, burning and damaging my right eye. It lost its sight and turned completely brown. After about a year, it had cleared up and my vision was returned. Because of lack of money, I never was medically treated for it. Today, it's slightly blurred.

— B.C. Ahouse

#105 – Friday December 1, 2000

During 1975, while at a NACD convention in Las Vegas, a friend, Ronald Thomson, of Seattle (I believe), invited me to have a beer with him and get acquainted with William Ruchehaus, the newly appointed head of the EPA. The meeting went very well and Bill invited me to consider a job with the EPA. My affairs hardly permitted it. Anyway, they both left after being joined by two of the finest looking 'ladies' I ever saw. On my later asking Ronald how he got away with it, he said, "My wife knows I am in good company when with Bill." Shortly after a woman joined me asking me to light her cigarette and join her in her room or mine, since she was a therapist.

I said that sure was a nice free offer.

She said, "Oh no, there is a price attached." I refused by telling her that my brother Al couldn't sleep if he knew someone in the family paid for it.

— B.C. Ahouse

#106 – Friday December 1, 2000

I wish to reflect on the greetings we received shortly after our arrival on the farm we bought from C. Lamoreau in 1945. We arrived here March 26, 1946. Being moved by my Uncle Richard Burman, who I paid with the last cash I had. A day or so later, our next-door neighbor, David Baker, showed up without saying hello. He demanded to know when I was going to fix my fence. I asked why? He said, "So my cows don't get out."

I said, "Isn't that your problem?"

He said, "No, it's yours."

I let this pass. Some time later, his wife, Anna Baker, stopped in to tell us of the customs of neighbors helping each other and that I would be expected to work at their threshing of oats. The chore they assigned me was to get into an enclosed space and level out the straw as it was blown in. Since I left the Army with respiratory problems, I said I couldn't and left with their condemnations. Joe Swarthout stopped and asked Irene if she would like some pears. Thinking it a gift, she said yes. Joe said, "That'll be $10.00." No sale.

—B.C. Ahouse

#107 – Friday December 1, 2000

I never heard of the annoyance called cluster flies until I came to Lodi, New York. Bob C. in Virginia calls them Army flies. They are the most insidious creatures God ever created. Once, at Cornell University, I asked a known entomologist if they could eradicate them. He asked, "Why? They are not an economic threat."

I said, "What are you talking about?" They are driving women crazy every year. These creatures show up in the early fall. They enter a house by crawling through the cracks between the window sash. Most die soon after and litter the floor. Some survive longer to buzz all winter long. Last year, 1999, they were very scarce because of the dry summer. This summer was wet and they made up for it without a doubt. From my house floors and from between the storm and house windows, I have removed at least two bushels of the critters.

—B.C. Ahouse

#107B – Friday December 1, 2002

I humorously set down this little ditty I coined about 40 years ago.

My little girl Nancy
Has a friend named Kim
And I think that she is
Quite fond of him
He is that nice young fellow
Who lives next door
In that big white house
With the flies on the floor.

It certainly wasn't my intent, but my regret. His mother Elsie Shoebridge saw that Ed her husband moved to New Jersey.

—B.C. Ahouse

#108 – Friday December 1, 2000

The situation at Mt. Climax was discussed at the 1975 NACD convention in Denver. Although I didn't intend to go to Lendville, a blizzard to the North of Colorado Springs prompted us to go west past Pike's Peak and into Lendville. We noticed the lunch sign at the Taberesurd Hotel for $2.50. We gladly went in. The food was homemade bread and Chinese Soup, which was OK. The bartender who admitted us said drinks were included. We asked for martinis. He said two for one. The soup and bread was delicious—we had no room for dessert, so he said how about two martinis? Mt. Climax was a huge peak, the mountain being almost 100% tailings. Mined in the past by shafts and tunnels, but now being excavated from the top, which was to the chagrin of some. One thing noticeable, my car, a 1972 Grand Marquis, had a tough time running at that altitude. I did investigate the mining situation and could only state in my brief that they won't miss a mountain around here.

—B.C. Ahouse

#109 – Saturday December 2, 2000

Since Irene, my wife, witnessed this little incident and saw the humor in it, I set it down. I was on the witness stand being questioned about some trivial matter. The situation became next to ridiculous and I simply said to the attorney, why be so 'Picky Lilly' about everything? He stood back a little and the court stenographer said, "Let's hold it. I don't know how to set down your word 'Picky Lilly.'" He was handwriting his notes. This occurred in Elmira, New York. The interrogation ceased.

—B.C. Ahouse

#110 – Saturday December 2, 2000

At the behest of William Pousoldt, I made contact with Donald Trump's man Tony Glidman with the purpose of buying Chalk Airline from Resorts International. Before it could be finalized, Trump sold Merv Griffin all the resorts except for the Taj Mahal in Atlantic City. I made acquaintance with Merv's CEO, David Hanlon, who said we would have to renegotiate the deal. Before this could be done, Resorts filed for bankruptcy, which squashed the whole deal. However, it led to complimentary rooms and meals at Resorts for Irene and I. Also a string of $5000.00-$25,000 jackpots for Irene and me. My associate Chuck Lucido said someone upstairs must be looking out for me. I quoted this to D. Hanlon and he said, "Bernie, it's higher than here."

—B.C. Ahouse

#111 – Saturday December 2, 2000

One evening in 1942, I happened to be in the Provost office in Ft. Belvoir with Pete Dailey, whose father was FDR's private chauffeur. I worked with Sam Savitts and Warren Pershing. The chauffeur's son Pete told tales out of the White House such as about FDR's girlfriend (nobody believed it then, including my mother-in-law Tillie). Sam, who was quite an artist, sketched Pershing and me sitting by his side. I said I'd like that, but Major Pershing claimed it. Then Sam did a sketch of a matador and a bull saying, "This is for a Taurus (me)." I located this picture in my wife's mail after 50 years and I framed it; it now hangs in my home. Pershing remarked that his young son was several weeks old, but he hadn't been to Washington to see him because he wouldn't pull rank. Someone did and I first saw his father, who drove out to pick him up. A neighbor of mine, Fuller, told me he was with this son in Vietnam when he was decapitated. Warren, who I had some contact with, then Pershing and Lewis, had a bad time. Heart operation and death followed this soon.

—B.C. Ahouse

#112 – Saturday December 2, 2000

During the '1970s, when business took us to NYC, we took in many shows. The handbills are probably upstairs. The best show in my opinion as a musical was *The Best Little Whorehouse in Texas*. It kept me awake. We saw it the second time when we took our son Karl and Darlene, his second wife, to see it. That night we walked to the Empire State Building and found Dar found out she was pregnant with Steve on the ride down the elevator. Incidentally, *The Best Little Whorehouse in Texas* was panned by the critics, but liked by the public. *Sweeny Todd*, with Brian Keith and Angela Lansbury, despite their good acting, was awful and I followed Irene in walking out midway. *Old Calcutta* with Rex Harrison, Claudette Culbert and one other put me to sleep even though I was in the front row chorus line. It was overrated in my opinion.

—B.C. Ahouse

#113 – Saturday December 2, 2000

When the head officer, Vern Alghren, of the Corning Savings and Loan told me to be thankful for their services because it wasn't profitable to lend to builders since speculating and other deals were more profitable, I then took notice of their business practices, which to me were not mandated in their charters. They also seemed to ignore the truth in the Lending Bill. Also, there was their refusal to abide by signed contracts. When in Florida, I went to the *National Enquirer's* office in Luntana and offered the story this matter encompassed. They just wouldn't believe what I was saying. I also went to the FBI office in the building where my friend David Bundy's office was in Geneva, New York. They said they took my tale to the Buffalo office and were told to ignore it. This was before the scandal broke that ruined my friend Bob Jacoby's son. He was the boy genius of banking. He ended up in Atlanta Federal Prison I think for the savings and loan scandal.

—B.C. Ahouse

#114 – Sunday December 3, 2000

The animal rights comrades have missed the largest case of brutality in the sexing of baby chicks. The day-old chicks have their genitals forced out, which allows an expert to determine the gender. To supply the great demand for laying hens, the females are carefully boxed for shipment—usually within one day. The cockerels are discarded monthly in an inhumane way by simply throwing them in a barrel to suffocate or drown if water is there. Some have other methods of destroying them.

I wish to record a very unusual matter. Gerwin Schaeffer, when he was hatching at Cold Springs Farm, merely dumped the cockerels into a gully along Seneca Lake on the Seneca County line. One day, Marvin Smith, who had a farmhouse about a half-mile from the dumpsite, heard a commotion on his side porch. Two starlings had just brought a still alive baby cockerel to his porch. Marvin took it in and warmed and fed it. The bird survived and lived to a ripe old age as Marvin's pet and cock of the walk.

—B.C. Ahouse

#115 – Sunday December 3, 2000

The Seneca Army Depot in Romulus, New York has a herd of remarkable white deer. They are not albinos, but through inbreeding because they are confined, they have reverted to an ancient coloring— their eyes are dark. The deer were exposed to controlled hunting by the State Wildlife Board and the Army. To bag a white buck was a hoped-for experience. The Townsend Hotel in Lodi—not the Eagle—allowed hunters to hang their trophies out front, probably for the advertising. Gus Sternvich shot a big brown buck and hung it as allowed. Russell Smith, a local joker, sprayed it with white paint, which Gus didn't appreciate. Some time later, Rus shot a big white buck and hung it in the same location. After the usual bragging in the bar, Rus went home (about two miles away). Someone soon called him and told him to get right down, that Gus was spraying his deer brown (actually he wasn't). Rus showed up immediately in his shorts and galoshes.

—B.C. Ahouse

#116 – Sunday December 3, 2000

It has been said that legal ethics are what a lawyer can get away with. When I was a boy, an old fellow warned me about saying hello to an attorney, for if I did, I'd never stop talking to them. Their clients' business is supposed to be confidential, but a Mr. Nicet bent my ear so much about others' business that I told him I was concerned about my own. After the Geneva Hospital Administrator told me to get a lawyer, I did. The simple agreement she wrote up allowed her to retain 30% after my expenses were deducted from the amount paid. Mr. Nicet often told me of his large contingencies of 33% off the top of his medical malpractice awards. He either did not know or did not care that he was robbing his clients. I have a canceled check to prove this. Also, he told me he was having State Senator Cherry pass some law so he could defraud his wife in a divorce settlement.

— B.C. Ahouse

#117 – Sunday December 3, 2000

Following the sale of most of our land to the Trust for Public Land, who immediately sold it to the U.S. Forest Service, we were constantly harassed by ridiculous phone calls — newspaper publicity — and finally, threatening phone calls. Many calls sounded like a witch giggling. On one occasion, John Carpenter, Senator Mike Nazzalio's assistant, called me to ask what I was complaining about. I said, "Which one? But why are you calling?" He said that I had left a threatening message on the recorder that morning. My son Martin came and went up to Seneca Falls, but John said he had erased it. I soon asked Former Senator Ted Day to visit me at my home. He did. I explained the situation, saying I was sure he was not behind this mischief, but he could probably find out. Whatever the reason, this crap stopped. It is now three and a half years later.

—B.C. Ahouse

#118 – Sunday December 3, 2000

I've seen some pretty disgusting things, but I will only note these two to illustrate that my life was not entirely full of pleasant happenings. Early in 1976, when I was in Honolulu on Waikiki Beach Park, I was approached by a bum who had his hair put up in probably a dozen spikes, each of which was inhabited by a cluster of lice on each end about the size of a green olive. The other happened in Covert, New York while I stopped at a gas and oil station with the family. There was an entrance room in the rear that I often entered and knocked on the door inside. There were ten or twelve full-sized cats outside the door. Without a thought, I opened it. The cats rushed inside to the large litter box all at once and relieved themselves. Phew!

—B.C. Ahouse

#119 – Monday December 4, 2000

The first job of any consequence that I held was in the winter of 1935-36, and it mainly involved shoveling snow on the new Jusup Central Railroad — the pay was 40 cents an hour. Beginning there and with every paycheck I received from the following employers — Link Brs., William Sutken, U.S. Army Corps, Halabud, U.S. Ensign Dept., Wall Street, New York City, and other short-term jobs — I gave my mother, Edith Ahouse, half of the paycheck, and while I was in the U.S. Army, she received $30.00 per month due to my contribution. After I was married and expecting a child, I terminated this practice. Much to the aggravation of my sister Ruth, who took me to task at Remington Rand, where I was instrumental in getting her a pretty good job. I wish to also state here that Irene and I provided my mother a home on Neal Road in Lodi, New York for 27 years. Never once did any of my siblings ask me how I was getting along. Some people thought the house was my mother's and that I would inherit it.

— B.C. Ahouse

#120 – Monday December 4, 2000

Mr. David Eichorn
TV Channel 9
Syracuse, NY 13200

Dear Mr. Eichorn!

I have been very cognizant of the weather since I spent several months during the winter of 1935-36 shoveling snow in zero-degree weather on the New Jersey Central Railroad as a teenager. I would like to run the following observations by you if I may. We (mostly) are aware of the tides in the ocean water caused by the gravitational effects of the sun and moon. I also view the atmosphere as an ocean of air which must have the same tidal effects. A depression would naturally be a low; a peak would be a high. Most meteorologists seem to imply that the jet stream moves the highs or lows. I believe the opposite, that the jet stream is the result of these areas.

Respectfully,
B.C. Ahouse

#121 – Monday December 4, 2000

When I was working out of the white building on Wall Street, a casual acquaintance remarked to me that I was going to hang around there to get into advertising or insurance. I asked him if I should insure advertisers or advertise insurers. He didn't answer. Also about this time, the colonel asked me if I'd like to see something very interesting. I asked who she was. He said it was nothing like that. We crossed the street, entered a bank building, and went downstairs to where the international gold holdings were juggled around, just like in Ft. Knox.

— B.C. Ahouse

#122 – Monday December 4, 2000

During the mid-1930s, times were very tough in the anthracite coalfields in Luzerne County, PA. The Glen Alden Coal Company, headed by a Major Inglase, paid in cash in those days. The Sugar Notch Colliery had the payroll delivered by the narrow-gauge railroad they owned to transport unprepared coal. Usually, this was done in an armored pay car. Big Mike, as the papers called him (I didn't know him personally), decided to share the wealth by blowing up the pay car. Everything went as planned except on this day an open coal car was used instead of the armored car. Instead of just blowing the car off the tracks, it demolished it, and the cash was blown over the hillside. When the word got out, everybody in the area got to gathering up the look. Heaven help you if the Coal and Iron Corps. caught you with any money. I was too late.

—B.C. Ahouse

#123 – Monday December 4, 2000

The New Jersey Central hauled coal to NY from Mountaintop, PA, where they had a yard called "Penobscot." The coal gondolas loaded with prepared coal were delivered to the yards by a system known as the Ashley Planes. This used a unique method whereby the pusher, which was activated by cable from above, would, by narrowing its wheels, drop under the four cars it was to push. This was made possible by a pit under the four cars. Actually, the cars were pushed not pulled, as some thought. There were three sets of these planes. They existed when I worked on the tracks in the late 'thirties and early forties. I was warned about the danger of the pits. By accident or by design, there was more than one Gandy dancer killed in them. The planes were removed in the 1950s I believe.

—B.C. Ahouse

#124 – Tuesday December 5, 2000

In early 1941, I was first exposed to asbestos while working as a carpenter at Ft. Holabird in Baltimore. This was when we gutted out a warehouse that originally belonged to Ballantine Brewery. No one knew of the potential damages and no protection was taken. Ft. Holabird was a quartermaster depot where various equipment was tested. There was an artificial mountain that was used as a test range. I saw and sat in the first Jeep before it was called a Jeep). The original engine was a V8 Ford, which proved too powerful—ripping up the transmission. This was replaced by a Willy's four cylinder, which proved satisfactory, and because the standard Jeep was named after a cartoon comic figure in Popeye.

—B.C. Ahouse

#125 – Tuesday December 5, 2000

About 20-some years ago, there was an article in the *Wall Street Journal* stating that the U.S. Dept. of Agriculture had made a deal with Cargill (the giant grain co.) whereby Cargill agreed to stop stealing from Watkins Salt. In realizing what they were talking about, I wrote a letter to the CEO of Cargill referring to said article and asking him if he would like to talk to me about it. Previously, we'd had some dialogue about moisture testers used in grain purchasers. He never answered. However, some time later, I was at a party in Watkins Glen. The head of Watkins Salt asked me to step outside. He simply said, "Bernie, be careful when you try to finger someone like the head of Cargill if you want to keep your health." He referred to my letter. I asked what the connection was. He told me Cargill was buying Watkins Salt from the Clause family.

—B.C. Ahouse

#126 – Tuesday December 5, 2000

In 1946, with a veterans' preference certified, I bought one tractor, one plow, one mower, one pulley, one buck rake, one tiller, and one buzz saw from Marion Boyce Ford Farm Dealer—all for the price of $900.00. This created some controversy with my neighbors, since these items were scarce and I was a newcomer. Over the years, I had many problems with new machinery. I bought three tractors that had an extra loose castle nut in the crankcase. Two I dismantled, one I didn't. They were all loose and extra. I bought a Massey Harris Tractor that because of its small traction wheels buried itself when in soft ground. Also a Massey Ferguson that on its first trip out almost upset itself when the lot arms holding the attached plow bent on the first turn, locking the wheels. This is just the beginning of what I will document about machinery.

— B.C. Ahouse

#127 – Wednesday December 6, 2000

On one occasion in 1941, in Baltimore after arriving there on a greyhound bus, I was taking a shortcut through a parking lot when a man approached me from behind, patting my rear pocket. I thought he might try to mug me, so I turned around, grabbed his coat, and asked what he wanted. He said, "A nip of what you should have on your hip." Another time in Montreal, I left my wife Irene and her mother Tillie in the underground to go to the men's room. These two young fellows followed me in, one of them crowding me at the urinal. The other stood with his back to the door. I pushed the one nearest aside and went up to the other asking him to step aside, or should I do it for him and maybe more? Since I showed no fear, I had no problem.

— B.C. Ahouse

#128 – Wednesday December 6, 2000

When I first appeared at the NYS Conservation District Board in Albany, I was plainly told if I went along, I'd get along. I tried that for a few months and honestly told them that I'd prefer to be myself. After I was politically edged out, Bill Carey's secretary told me that my three years there were the most interesting to him. Before I left, Bill Carey nominated me to be (I took it as the token farmer) on the Tri-Lateral Commission. I appeared in NYC at their office and was thoroughly questioned. I didn't think David Rockefeller was sanctioning me. So, when I was asked if I understood the purpose of their organization, I said probably it was the method by which the Rockefellers would line up the world to their liking. I wasn't accepted.

— B.C. Ahouse

#129 – Wednesday December 6, 2000

About 25 years ago, Irene's half-brother Joe Brieker Sr. passed away. His mother Tillie Olson held his note for $10,000; the lawyer for the estate told her to get a lawyer to talk to him. She asked me if I knew a good one in Baltimore. I told her no. Often listening to her problem, I said, "If you trust me, just sign the note over to me and I'll take care of it." She did. Joe Jr. wanted her to have the money, but the lawyer stalled. I went to Baltimore, called the lawyer and told him I'd be in to talk to him. When I arrived, he told me that he didn't know if I was qualified to talk to him. I simply said, "I'll give you two minutes to decide." I must have been qualified because it didn't take much dialogue to receive the amount, and Tillie got her money. She gave me a considerable stipend.

—B.C. Ahouse

#130 – Thursday December 7, 2000

It's 59 years since Pearl Harbor was attacked. I was at Uncle Bill Brush's home when the radio brought the news. It sure changed many things. One thing that I must set down is when Leonard Kitlinski came to Fort Belvoir O.C.S. and we renewed our acquaintance. (We were friends in Nanticoke and when he went into the Army, I bought his 1932 Chevrolet Sedan for $90.00.) Leonard assured me that this fact is true, that on the morning of December 7, 1941 as the chauffeur for General Shorts, he drove him up on the Diamond Head to watch the Japs come in. The general was distressed.

— B.C. Ahouse

#131 – Friday December 8, 2000

In 1959, because of the many families with a Lutheran background who were not attending any church services, a group of members—myself, Bernard Ahouse, Alfred Ahouse, Rubert Subol, Lloyd Koke, and Carl Gleisner—banded together and petitioned the Mission Board of the Missouri Synod, who provided support through Reverend Donald Schroeder. We were joined by others, including William Sonutag, Anne Hamilton, Gilbert Smith, Hannes Henoven, and were able to purchase the All Saints Episcopal Church, which was in private hands, for the low price of $1350.00. A loan being made at the Wheeler National Bank, with Myron Bassett handling it. As with any joint venture, various problems occurred, but God was with Christ Lutheran Church, and it has now survived for over 40 years.

—B.C. Ahouse

#132 – Friday December 8, 2000

About ten years ago, I lost my large barn to a fire. I wish to catalog the following events:

1. A stiff wind was blowing from the south.
2. Early in the morning, I burned off the weeds around the pond across the road, 100 feet to the north. It burned out.
3. A couple loaded hay from the barn, and by their letter testified that there was no fire near to the barn.
4. The NYSEG Electric Pole, rotten at the bottom, broke but did not fall immediately.
5. A year earlier, a neighbor, Paul Shoff, dropped a tree and took down the power line. It also broke near said pole and was patched.
6. The swaying pole caused the patch to break and the line fell on the northeast corner of the barn, setting it afire. It burned a deep mark in the lawn up to the barn, which was visible for weeks later.
7. My neighbor, Harry James, lost power before the fire whistle sounded after I called the Fire Company.
8. Mike Allen and Bill Trim were the first firemen here. Mike foolishly cut the dangling line in front of my house. Irene saw him, but he was not hurt.

9. The first words on the videotape were "where is the power company? We have lines coming down," by Billy Palmer.

10. The heat from the barn was terrific, but it did not melt the aluminum roof on the silo attached to the barn. NYSEG said at court the line was burned off.

11. Bob Champion was here. He removed 1976 Mercury Marquis from the barn.

12. The entire fire was videotaped.

13. In Judge Sirocense's court when being played, the TV power went off, and he wouldn't allow it to be shown later.

14. The couple loading hay were not subpoenaed by my attorney — Nicet. He said NYSEG called them. They never showed.

15. Danny Simmon showed late at the fire and at court. He lied, saying he removed the 1976 Mercury. He didn't, Bob did.

16. I also think he saw the land had burned up to the barn. The fact is that the barn fire burned the lawn, which surrounded the entire barn.

17. At court, Billy Palmer said that he meant the lines were going to come down.

— B.C. Ahouse

#133 – Friday December 8, 2000

Early in 1942, I went to Bush Terminal in Brooklyn New York and applied for a job as a carpenter. It appeared that there was some confusion in the direction of shipments overseas. The first job there was for a German immigrant, scientist, to build a lab bench. He took great offense to me for some unknown reason. I made acquaintance with some young fellows who took me into their confidence, probably thinking I was one of them. They were a very well organized communist cell and made no bones about it, while maintaining the Americanism. I chided them about not being in the Army. How they kept out, I don't know, but they said they were contributing more to their cause where they were. One point they made clear was when they bragged about Stalin just sending John Reed a cool million dollars cash. My reports were not taken seriously.

– B.C. Ahouse

#134 – Friday December 8, 2000

At Quaker Maid in Bush Terminal, there was a new machine to make cellophane bags for jellybeans that wouldn't work. I fixed it by roughing up the manipulating arm. Incidentally, the jellybeans were coming out dusty or dull. The beans were made on the top floor and dropped through a shoot, where they were sprayed with sugar liquid. The dust was coming from a spaghetti drier which I vented through the roof to eliminate the problem. The spaghetti came out of the drier onto a conveyor line where numerous women manually weighed the required amount and put it in the proper container. I noted that one lady very seldom had to add or subtract from her first handful. I commented to her about it, and she simply said that it was because it was about the same size as her boyfriend's dick.

—B.C. Ahouse

#135 – Friday December 8, 2000

I first became aware of Henry Mencken in 1941 while working in Baltimore. I recall one barb to him by a student about Mencken Augustinianism. What would you do if you found yourself facing St. Peter at the Golden Gate? I'd admit I was wrong.

— B.C. Ahouse

#136 – Friday December 8, 2000

In early 1942, when with the USED on Wall Street, I was told to go over to Camp Kilmer, NJ and apply for a job as a carpenter. As I viewed the situation, there was a shortage of labor in NJ and an apparent surplus in NY. However, Northern NJ was controlled by Frank Hague, the mayor of Newark, and he wasn't willing to accommodate Republican NY—him being a democrat. Anyway, I showed up as directed—I was thoroughly interrogated and poorly treated. In any respect, I didn't get a job but was locked up in a closet overnight. I haven't thought much of the Democrats since. My brother Morgan, however, is a NJ Democrat.

—B.C. Ahouse

#137 – Friday December 8, 2000

While at DPC plant Remington in 1943 in Johnson City, NY, as supervisors, we had what was called a safety meeting every week. These included other matters as when we were introduced to the rural plan. The Desert Fox came to mind, but this was much more destructive to our way of life. But what came up in our introduction was the mechanics by which the women in the war effort would be kept working to provide more taxes and also supplement the loss of that money. I don't believe the returning veterans relished the thought of their wives being held in to the workforce. In any respect, social planning took one big bite out of our lifestyle.

—B.C. Ahouse

#138 – Saturday December 9, 2000

While Irene was in intensive care at Geneva General Hospital, the social worker, a Ms. McCarthy, called me into her office to criticize me for having an evening martini with my wife, saying that was why she was in the state she was in. I said that it was legal and we didn't overdo it. At 2:00 a.m., while Irene was still there, I got a call saying it was GGH, which scared me. It was her again, saying she hoped I didn't have a martini last evening. She also had her staff hound me too. The following May 1995, she was in Rochester to make a purchase of cocaine for her group and was murdered by a man for the money he knew her to be carrying. This all came out in court and was well publicized. My question... Who was her group?

—B.C. Ahouse

#139 – Saturday December 9, 2000

About 10 years ago or so, a Dr. Grey Mickalecoher moved next door on the Sablor farm, which he bought and subsequently tried to get back to the land and raise sheep. I tried to be a good neighbor, as did my son Martin. I ended up paying for some of their fertilizer bills. Anyway, I liked the man and received a good insight into the Willard Psychiatric Hospital. He became engaged to my friend, John D.'s, daughter and I was the only local invited to his stag party, which was comprised of about ten to twelve of his doctor friends from around the U.S. A tall good-looking man was introduced to me as the best surgeon in Seattle, Washington. As I was helping them drink their bourbon, this man passed me a container of white powder and an ear scraper, saying, "Have some." I refused. He said, "Come on then you can rap at our level."

I said, "If I can't, let me know and I'll leave."

—B.C. Ahouse

#140 – Saturday December 9, 2000

In the middle of 1978, after eating a large spinach salad, I ended up in the ER of Schuyler Memorial Hospital. My friend, Dr. Nick Anastasia, said I had a kidney stone lodged in my urethra and a Dr. Abeyatongrea would remove it with a Schwartz basket. I said I'd sooner go home and drink a couple of six packs to flush it out. He and my wife Irene persuaded me to stay. I woke up after the process with a large incision on my left side and a drainage bag attached to it. Several years later because of my friend Dr. G. Micklachev's interest, we went to the hospital and learned what had happened. Dr. Abeyatongrea went too far up the urethra and couldn't retract it. No stone. To remove the instrument, he had to cut me open and remove it backwards. I contracted a severe infection. I went to Dr. R. Meyer in Ithaca, who criticized me for going to that quack Dr. Abeyatongrea, who was not a urologist at all. Meyer put me on sulfur pills and told me to take a long rest. I recovered but had the incision repaired by a Dr. Seymour Schmarks, but to no good avail.

— B.C. Ahouse

#141 – Saturday December 9, 2000

I was honorably discharged from the U.S. Army late in June 1945 in fair health but with an excellent character. I checked back with the USED on Wall Street. I was directed to the defense plant of Remington Rand, the Propelling Division in Johnson City, NY. I practically walked into a position on the Lands External Grinder, which ground two bearing surfaces. There was a problem with the process with neither bearing surface being concentric with the 360 degree Hypord gear on the rotary cam. I almost immediately saw the problem. The cam was installed on an arbor which went between the points of the grinder bed. The opening in the gear end was rough ground. When the large washer was inserted and hammered tight with a large nut, it distorted the whole cam. Although the bearing was OK while on the arbor, it lost its original shape when removed. I went to the plumbing shop and made a larger rafter to cushion the washer.

– B.C. Ahouse

#141A – Saturday December 9, 2000

To remedy the distortion, the plant had 20 or more women filing the bearing's high spots until they became concentric. This was a slow and costly process. When I solved this matter, I was on the nightshift. When the day shift came in, there wasn't any need for the women workers, which annoyed the supervisor, a John Lujok. He called the plant engineer, a Mr. Meyer, who asked, "What is going on?" He was told that Ahouse had solved the problem. He was furious. He met me when I came in and told me that I was fired. I asked why. He said I changed the process without engineering approval.

I went into the colonel's office and simply said, "I will probably see you again."

He asked, "What's going on?"

I told him. He called Meyers, listened to his story, and then fired him. The colonel then asked if I'd like to stay till the war was over, I said yes.

—B.C. Ahouse

#141B – Saturday December 9, 2000

After the episode with the colonel, I was given a position in supervision as an assistant foreman with a good paying income. The women on the file bench became a problem, but they were kept on the payroll, but with their idle time, they became a source of complaints. I thought they would be reassigned, but in the meantime, they complained of various illnesses. To be proper, I sent them to the plant doctor, a Dr. DeAngelo, who called me for sending him a constant stream of patients who he said weren't sick. I said, "You're the doctor." After a few days, their illnesses ceased. I asked the doctor how he cured them. He simply said he took the two best lookers, told them to disrobe, get on the examining table, and they had a couple of security men walk by.

— B.C. Ahouse

#143 – Sunday December 10, 2000

The LaPointe Broache on the spider line that made the final cut for the space between the spider and the barrel always finished with chatt in mark. I turned the hydraulics pressure up to the limit (beyond specs), and it came out like polished glass. The Tocco heat treatment machine, which worked through magnetic induction, heated the stop lug ring that went into the stationary com. Oil was squirted on it to harden it. The problem was the half-inch copper tubing that conducted the heat periodically exploded. I noticed that when someone was drinking from a nearby fountain, the explosion happened. Obviously, the water as a coolant in the tubing was diminished. And the overheating caused the problem. A direct supply of water solved the problem.

—B.C. Ahouse

#143A – Sunday December 10, 2000

I recall another meeting I had with the colonel; I believe to set me up. Lujok had two men come to work on Saturday to catch up some production on the spider line. They appeared in their finest clothes as though planning something other than working. After some heated discussion, I told them to either go to work or get the fuck out. They hauled me before a union board and accused me of improper conduct. The colonel asked me if I said such and why? I said yes, because I thought I was talking to a couple of men. After Veterans' Day, the colonel came to me and told me to get a hammer and destroy the brimmed/rockwell and video testing devices. I protested. He showed me a letter from the U.S. government promising that they would not be put on the market but destroyed at the war's end. I truly destroyed tens of thousands of dollars that evening. Incidentally, he also told me that I would be approved for the piecework bonus plan retroactively.

—B.C. Ahouse

#144 – Sunday December 10, 2000

1. On Thursday December 7, 2000, I attended the funeral services for Arthur Utter Jr., who had committed suicide. He just couldn't handle the problems he created for himself. He was a victim of the political and economic correctness of our defunct schools and banks that seem to overwhelm people.
2. Years ago, Lloyd Champion, because of unjust criticism of his kin, hanged himself. He had just told me that he was going down to the lake to jump in. I told him I'd go too.
3. James Norton shot himself in my 1970 mercury after being hounded by the sheriff's department in Seneca County for something I am sure he wasn't involved in.
4. Bill Coater jumped off the Mill Creek Bridge one half-mile south of Lodi and killed himself. He was always short of money. I was away at the time and couldn't loan him any.
5. Darrel Trureiss shot himself in his car on Butcher Hill Road in fear of again being charged with juvenile sexual abuse by the Lodi sheriff.
All of these men worked for me at different times.

          —B.C. Ahouse

#145 – Sunday December 10, 2000

I mention my dad, Bernard 'Victor' Ahouse, in his *Nipped in the Bud*. He was a gifted artist and before he lost his right arm, he became a tattoo artist, granting tattoos to all of his friends to the anger of their mothers. This was about 1890. He lost his arm on March 17, 1875, and after the amputation (for which he got $60), he developed the same skills with his left hand. Although he was a teacher of pianoforte and the piano, he left a legacy in his artwork. One of the reasons I left the army in 1943 was to get him out of the psychiatric hospital at Ranson, PA. It didn't work out with his being back home, and he went to NJ, where my brother Morgan was. His health caused him to leave his job, and he came back to the Johnson City area. For a while, he stayed with Irene and I, but because of the crowding, I got him a room in town. While there, I encouraged him to do some color carbon drawings. Three Currier and Ives of a hunter camping out, and one half complete railroad in Sierra. He completed each detail from right to left. There was also a decoy on a bench. Dog to Chipper. Flowers to Millie. I treasure these pictures, and only regret that we weren't closer through his life. He died in 1945.

—B.C. Ahouse

#146 – Sunday December 10, 2000

When I attended Washington Street School in Nanticoke, PA, my sister Olga came down with scarlet fever and was quarantined at home. Ruth and I were kept out of school. Her books and ours were burned. However, I had a Winston simplified dictionary, property of Nanticoke public schools, dated September 1, 1925 at home. I still have it in my hand on my desk as I write this one memory that recurs when I eat an apple. It's how when someone else had an apple, we'd follow him around asking for the core. Things were very different in those days. One event that seems humorous but wasn't to the two who perpetuated it. Two boys, recent immigrants from Eastern Europe, started school with us (neither of them speaking any English). There was a convenient store kitty-corner from the school owned by Jureks. These boys stole a box from a delivery truck and thinking it chocolate, ate the entire box, which contained a laxative. They were easy to catch.

—B.C. Ahouse

#147 – Sunday December 10, 2000

I can't miss telling about my mother's mother, Lena Rachel Brush Burman. With her family, she immigrated from Pomerania or East Prussia on the Russian border in Germany in the 1880s. She had six children with her first husband, Carl Brush. One son, Charles, was born in Oklahoma when my mother was eight years old. Her father, Carl, was killed by rock fall in the Bliss Colliery of the Glenn Alden Coal Company. In sympathy, the company delivered his body to Grandma and left him on the porch. Compare this situation to the plight of the slaves which is getting much attention. Now Grandma then married Leopold Burman, who was a brother-in-law to her in-laws. She had six children, three boys and three girls—the same as by Carl Brush. Leopold broke his leg by the foolish tactic of making a fire out of rye straw when removing rocks from the family farm. Stepson Charles told him to twist the straw, but he didn't and when lit, it set off the dynamite.

—B.C. Ahouse

#148 – Sunday December 10, 2000

While at the hospital in Fort Hamilton, I met a noncom from the Cameron Highlanders of the British Army. His name was George Brown and we, Irene and I, became quite attached to him. George was standing guard on a troop transport coming to the U.S. when he witnessed a near miss on the bow by a German torpedo. In his fright, thinking it would explode directly below him, he lost his voice, and we communicated by writing and gestures. He gave me his officer whistle, a thunderer, which he said was all he took with him when he left Dunkirk and started to swim the Channel. He was picked up halfway across. He said, "Blow it when you come, and I won't put the dogs on you." My son Karl lost it while playing in the yard in about 1950. I found it with my Houston metal detector 30 years later. The ring had rusted off, the cork in it was intact, and it still blows like new.

—B.C. Ahouse

#149 – Monday December 11, 2000

My mother, Edith Ahouse, moved into the Neul house, which I remodeled somewhat to make her comfortable. After nine or ten years, I was audited by the IRS and told that I owed $8000 in taxes and penalties. I asked why? I was told I couldn't deduct anything on the Neul house because my mother was my dependent. I said, "That's not so. I never claimed her as a dependent." They asked why she didn't pay me rent. I told them she had no money to do so.

I was asked, "If she did, and wouldn't, what would you do?"

I said, "Put her out on the road."

Shortly after, a social worker showed up and qualified my mother for supplemental social security in the amount of $100 per month so that it could take care of my expenses. Mom gave me the $100 monthly, which I entered as income, much to the criticism of my sisters, who never questioned the burden on me and my wife.

—B.C. Ahouse

#150 – Monday December 11, 2000

During the early 1990s, in negotiating with the trust for public land regarding the sale of most of our land, which was necessitated by the pressure of the farm credit systems, a proper appraisal was necessary. The trust engaged a firm from the Weschester County area at huge expense who didn't even come close. They then hired John Hovemeyer, of Syracuse, NY, who left it up to a newly arrived person from London, England, who did no better. The Forest Service was disturbed, so I said to Jim Allen, of Vermont, "Why can't you do it properly with the aid of the Romulus School District appraisals?" He did, came up with a satisfactory figure based on this other appraisal, and purchases were made.

—B.C. Ahouse

#151 – Monday December 11, 2000

During my tenure on County and State Conservation Boards, I heard many complaints:

1. A Mrs. Sullivan in complaining about the water quality of Cayuga Lake said, "When I moved there, you could drink the water. Now it froths with detergents." I said, "Mrs. Sullivan, I believe you have just indicted yourself."

2. When the Loran Tower was proposed on the Seneca Army Depot, I heard many complaints and acknowledged them all. But said they missed my chief concern, society could zero in on it.

3. A group came to Albany asking our board for support in their "Corn for the World. No meat for us" proposition. I was called inconsiderate in my saying farmers are doing more than most to relieve hunger. When asked what I would support, I said, "I'd teach all who would listen how to make a pot of soup and then I'd show them how to clean the pot."

—B.C. Ahouse

#152 – Monday December 11, 2000

Bill Long of Fayette, a Seneca County board member brought to our attention the fact that NY farmers had no claim on the state water for agriculture, and he proposed a statute creating such claim on Seneca Lake. When the word got out, the NYSGE appeared with the lawyers and engineers claiming that they had title to about eight feet of water say between 600-608 feet of elevation. I jokingly said we would only remove water below that level. Nothing ever became of Bill's God Plan. On another occasion, Seneca Co. Board was asked to support application for a nuclear power plant called Bell Station next to Milliken Station on Cayuga Lake. The board approved the plan, and I signed it with my concern that when it was obsolete, what? I was told by that time, the technology would be available to take care of it. I said, "If it isn't, you should all be hanged."

— B.C. Ahouse

#153 – Monday December 11, 2000

About 30 to 40 years ago, three men Charly Treman, president of Thompkins County Trust Co., J.S. Bair, with Pershing and Jewes Wall Street, and my friend Leo Bell came here to my home to introduce me to and speculate in the stock market. I am sure that their intent was good, and I accepted their plan. The TCTC even loaned me money, which I was assured would never be higher than 5% interest. I don't believe I lost any money, but neither did I make any because of the times. Tobin Bucking is another matter that I'll write about later. In retrospect, I probably would have been best off to let J.S. Bair Co. handle the investments at their responsibility.

— B.C. Ahouse

#154 – Monday December 11, 2000

During November 1994, I missed two insider stock purchases. They would have been very profitable. By the middle of the month, David Hanlon said if I chose, this was the time to buy Resorts Inc. It was about 75 cents. Irene ended up in Geneva General Hospital and the trauma of it all allowed this possibility to escape my mind. It finally sold for $8-$9, I believe. After Irene was home, Dr. Fred Fist called me to mention a Syntrol Inc. stock, an animal pharmaceutical company that was going to be taken over by a large company. It was for pennies. But Irene's state didn't allow her to consider it. Dave Bair provided info and when we, Irene and I, last visited his office, he suggested we buy 10,000 shares at $2.50. Irene walked out and we didn't. I believe it went over ten dollars.

— B.C. Ahouse

#155 – Tuesday December 12, 2000

Ben Brown was an executive of Maritime Mills, a feed company in Buffalo, NY. I first met him when he sold some lake property to John Hagopion of Binghamton, who I worked for in Binghamton. No one else would sell to John because he was Lebanese. Ben Fist introduced me to Southern Comfort. When I was doing the plumbing work on Pulver's cottage, the Pink Passion Pit, Ben's grandchildren (their father was an army colonel) often came over to visit—a boy and a younger sister. One time their mother came to me seeking her daughter. The boy was quiet. I helped her look, but to no avail. She called the police, who showed up with the fire company and other volunteers. The lake was searched. I went back to work since enough people were searching. About quitting time, the boy came to me, and I casually said without thinking, "Let's find your sister."

He said, "OK," and led me to an outside toilet further up the slope where he had locked her in.

—B.C. Ahouse

#156 – Tuesday December 12, 2000

Dr. Harold Fuller, a veterinarian of Interlaken, took care of and artificially bred our cows when we were in the dairy business. One day while in the barn, he thoroughly looked over one of the barn cats and then asked me if he could borrow it. That was a new one to me. I said yes, and he left with it. Sometime later, he returned the cat in good condition without any explanation. One night at the Masonic Lodge in Interlaken, I asked if he would explain that strange matter to me. He said about two months before that incident, a lady from Delaware ran over a cat by Hunts Barn and brought it to him and left it there with 50 dollars. The cat couldn't be saved. He then got a call from the lady asking about the cat which he said was fine. She said she would stop to see it, and she did, and she left another 50 dollars. No split to me.

—B.C. Ahouse

#157 – Tuesday December 12, 2000

Early in 1976, I happened to be in the Seaport Inn in Lafina Maui, Hawaii with my friend Rodney Sellers, who had just ordered an after-dinner drink of Tia Maria. When delivered he protested that it was Kahlua. The bartender came over and said, "You are right," and sent us a full bottle of Tia Maria. I went to the bar to thank him and spoke to an older couple. They were interrupted by their hippie son who stepped between me and his father. I said, "Sonny, you are kind of rude."

He said, "If you don't like me now, smell my armpit," and he lifted his arm.

Noticing his bare feet, I came down hard on them with the heel of my shoe.

Back at the table, there was some loud dialogue. Someone came over asking who had that distinguishing voice. When I spoke, he said, "You do. I am Francis Ford Coppola, you could replace John Wayne. If you come to Hollywood, we'll screen test you."

Knowing my wife would never believe that, I declined.

— B.C. Ahouse

#158 – Tuesday December 12, 2000

While on Maui, Rod Sellers and I decided to drive around Maui in my rented Toyota. We were also checking out some proposed sites. The local electricity generators were unique. I experienced my first six-dollar six-pack of Heineken beer. At Kipahula we viewed Lindbergh's grave on the left side of the road by a church. At the Seven Veil Falls, a lady kindly told us of the Hawaiian marriage tradition. If a fellow could consummate a sexual encounter below each falls between sunrise and sunset on the same day, he was eligible for the marriage, that's what she said.

The next mile or two were harrowing being on a one-lane road with a hundred-foot drop to the sea. No guardrail. We made it and didn't encounter a lot until we got down to the level. Our next stop was at a very well constructed church said to be a hundred years or older and in excellent condition. In the cemetery, I prevented some tourists from chipping off a mosaic portrait of the man buried there. I was amazed by the honeycomb-like appearance in the distant hillside. Upon examining it, I discovered it to be about 80 square garden sites (said to be a Puritan work ethic) surrounded by cleared rock. The stone fences were overgrown with vines to give its appearance.

—B.C. Ahouse

#159 Thursday December 14, 2000 –

In the middle 1970s, while in Las Vegas at the NACD Convention, I made the acquaintance of a Hank Greenspan, who was the publisher of the local newspaper. He elaborated on a legal problem which I recall as such: He was sued for libel by a person for one million dollars. His insurance company thought he was at fault, but he didn't. The insurance company told Hank they would pay the one million. Hank would not agree. The impasse led to the company giving Hank the one million and wiping their hands of it. After several years, Hank still had the one million and it sounded like he'd keep it. Years later, an ex-employee of his, Aaron Stevens, told me he probably did.

— B.C. Ahouse

#160 – Thursday December 14, 2000

About 1973, I had a brief business relationship with a Glen Treadwell to build a house for him. He managed the Lumps Restaurant for his family in Horseheads, NY. His relative, as I heard it, sold the Lumps Corp. of Miami and bought the Caesar's in Las Vegas. When I was in Vegas a few years later, I had reason to see Glen Treadwell. So, I went over to the Tropicana one evening. I approached a security person and asked if he could direct me to Glen Treadwell, who I believed was working there. The guard told me to stay right here. Shortly, two burly men came to me and said, "How would you like to see Frank Sinatra?" They escorted me to a front row seat. They stood by until the show was over, and they showed me to the front door. I never did see Glen.

—B.C. Ahouse

#161 – Thursday December 14, 2000

Some minor incidents pop up to mind like the few I'll mention here. One night in South Carolina, we were in a pizza place and ordered a large pizza. My wife saying, "But no oregano."

The pleasant young waitress simply said, "I don't know that white word."

Another time in Clearwater, Florida, I ordered a chocolate milkshake, but I wanted it made with vanilla ice cream. The waitress adamantly said, "How in the hell are you going to get a chocolate shake with vanilla ice cream?"

SYRUP

One night in a French restaurant in Haerohi, Atlantic City, we ordered a before-dinner wine, which the steward sampled to me. I sniffed it and simply said, "It is no good."

He was amazed, saying, "I don't know what to do since no one has ever said that to me before."

—B.C. Ahouse

#162 – Thursday December 14, 2000

Over the years, I gradually got a legal education as follows. For one example, in about 1960, I bought a farm adjoining our farm from Anton and Guchun Twedt. They carried a Duchane money mortgage. At one point, a barn was destroyed by wind and I received a payment of, I believe, $1500.00. Deeming it proper, I gave it to the Twedts, thinking I had taken care of my yearly payment. Without any advance notice, I received a foreclosure notice from their attorney Arthur Golden of Trumansburg. I went to his office, and he told me that the payment I made was applied to the tail end, not currently, and the foreclosure stood. I went next door to the Tompkins Co. Trust Co., borrowed the full amount due and paid him off.

—B.C. Ahouse

#163 – Saturday December 16, 2000

Most children have had a bicycle during their youth, but I never did. The fad today seems to be scooters. In the late 1920s, I did have a scooter, but I didn't have it for long. It was stolen from off our back porch on Washington Street in Nanticoke, PA. I never found out who took it. However, I also had a coaster wagon used to bring the coal home that I scavenged on the waste bank of the Bliss Colliery. This was one event that my father, Bernard, and I did together, but I mostly did it alone. The Bliss Colliery was the mine where my grandfather, Carl Brush, was killed in 1890 by a fall of coal.

—B.C. Ahouse

#164 – Saturday December 16, 2000

Not much has been written about mine cave-ins from the surface, but I recall a few. About 1927, my parents' family were all returning from Grandma Burman's farm in Bovance. We boarded the "Cannonball" (the electric train from Wilkes Barre to Hazelton) in Mangola. The train stopped suddenly on the north side of the tunnel on the verge of a very deep cave-in. We walked on the edge of the cove hole down to Sugar Notch and took the streetcar home to Barney Street. I recall how good the chipped beef and toast tasted after that cold walk. Another time, the public school building (a square brick affair about three floors) suffered a cave in and a quarter of the building fell into the mines. The coal company did replace it with a long low building in Sheatown near the New Jersey Central Railroad.

— B.C. Ahouse

#165 – Saturday December 16, 2000

During the fall of 1941, I was courting my wife Irene Lentz, who lived near Mangola. I had a 1937 Ford two-door sedan, which was my transportation. One night near midnight, I was coming down the Newport Mountain below Fairchild Pond, approaching Alden, when I noticed a darkness in the road ahead of me. I stopped and walked down to an enormous cave hole. I turned my car around to stop traffic. The first guy thought I was trying to hold him up, but he turned grateful when he saw what was ahead. I drove up to the Rushins Store at Fairchild and called the police. Another time at the mine near Alden, a 300-foot section of the New Jersey Railroad caved in. Disaster was prevented by a miner coming from Bliss Colliery. He crawled over the cave on the rails and alerted the train due in a few hours. (He was awarded a one-way pass to NYC.)

—B.C. Ahouse

#166 – Sunday December 17, 2000

About 40 some years ago, Bill Wagner (the present founder and owner of Wagner Vineyards) and I were in a minstrel show in Lodi Masonic Hall. Bill was a black dandy and I was a colored mammy. We sang several songs including *You, You, You*, which we dedicated to a local sheepherder, but no one picked up the point. My wife Irene made a large moo moo dress for me and stuffed my breast and rear with pillows. My face was black. Just when I was ready to leave, Bill McCoy came to my door pleading with me to pull him out of the ditch where he ran his truck. I said, "Hey, no." He said to just get a tractor and he'd hook everything up. This he did and I had just pulled him back into the road when two state troopers drove up. One shined a light on my black face and costume and exclaimed, "Now I've seen everything!"

— B.C. Ahouse

#167 – Monday December 18, 2000

Late July 1942, I left Ft. Jay NYC on a troop train, a long roundabout ride hotter than hell, locked in tight. I arrived at Ft. Dix later in the day. Everybody lined up. First refreshment of the day on the dock, an orange and a bottle of milk. I believe everybody threw up in unison. We were then herded up to a large hall where we took the regulation I.Q. and mechanical adaptability tests. I don't believe that I completed 80% of them, but I scored 145 on the I.Q. and 154 on the mechanical adaptability. Irene came to visit me the second Sunday I was there, when we were allowed visitors. Without delay, they then called us in for short aim inspection and to police up the area.

– B.C. Ahouse

#168 – Monday December 18, 2000

In the late 1970s, my sons Martin and Karl made contact with a group who were contemplating a rock festival, Woodstock II. I had very little to do with it except to give my approval. Eventually, I ended up in the Schuyler Hospital during most of the negotiations. My associate, Charles a. Lucedo worked with them and arrived at a contract, I believe the principal backer was CBS. The greyhound bus delivered the package and Chuck cut out the dollar figures. As I recall, we were to receive a quarter of a million provided that the Lodi town board approved, whether it materialized or not. If it did, us and the town would receive one million. The town supervisor, Francis Hard, first approved, then didn't because of pressure from Ovid Supervisor Larry Wilkins and Covert Supervisor Carl Swanson. Those two wanted our million. They got the county board to pass a resolution preventing gatherings of over 5000 people, which essentially killed the project.

– B.C. Ahouse

#169 – Monday December 18, 2000

I became acquainted with Major Edwin Horde at Mitchell Field in 1942 while he was biding his time of six months until he could pick up his commission after just returning from China. As he related to me, he was the youngest of a large family from Titusville PA. His father being one of the original oil millionaires from the strike in Pennsylvania. I recall his quoting his father as saying, "When all I had was a good big family, the world left me alone, but after the wealth came, the world kept knocking at my door." To isolate Edwin from the family fortunes, he was sent to San Francisco under the tutelage of a family friend. He was also sent a modest amount of money, hoping to teach Ed frugality. His tutor, however, invested the cash in some vacant property which soon soared in value, making Edwin wealthy on his own.

— B.C Ahouse

#170 – Monday December 18, 2000

Major Horde told me that he was in command of a unit of the American Expeditionary Force that entered Russia at Murmansk after the Bolsheviks took control. His outfit traveled the Trans-Siberian Railroad to Vladivostock and Port Arthur on the Pacific. He related the bad conduct of some of his troops, like wantonly machine-gunning Siberian towns. Also about the anal health problems of his troops, and his effort to get them to keep clean. He also told me of a deal he had with the Red Communists whereby they sent his cement to china after he settled there in the contracting business. The best part of the cement deal was the gold dust he removed once it was in China. He also related to me about a contract he made with one city where he took the night soil contract as collateral. I asked what it was. He said the overhead sewer system of China. People set out their toilet pots, and a coolie picked it up and expertly tossed it into an open tanker without spilling a drop.

— B.C. Ahouse

#171 – Tuesday December 20, 2000

Early in 1941, William Saint Kim and I were going to Baltimore, MD to seek work in the defense construction effort. I was driving his 1930 Chevrolet two-door sedan. Just North of Harrisburg, I believe on Route 11, we ran into icy conditions. I was going down a modest incline when I became aware of traffic problems ahead. An Army convoy had hit the ice and piled into each other along with a Greyhound bus. Just as I thought I would too, I saw an entrance to a field on the right and I avoided an accident by running off into said field, where we spent some time. There were, I was told, fatalities among the Army personnel. When we got to Baltimore, I was quite late, and we went into a tourist home, thinking to spend the night. We couldn't have been in bed for an hour when Bill woke me up slapping the bugs off himself. The sheet was riddled with blood spots. We left, but got no refund.

— B.C. Ahouse

#172 – Thursday December 21, 2000

When we started the dairy on the farm, some 50 years ago, I also bought some Angus cattle from Don MacIntock and a bull from the Grubes Bros. of Ovid. These grew into a sizable herd, and in the need of money, I sold them to Lester Crouch. He had Bill Dodge pick them up and moved them to Bill's farm, South of Mecklenburg. Sometime later, I ran into Lester in the Wheeler National Bank in Interlaken, and he said he might as well straighten up for our cattle deal, and he did. I was at the Tompkins Co. Hospital in Ithaca a short time later, and I learned that Lester was a patient there. I went to his room to visit him and thank him. At the door, a nurse told me that Mr. Crouch had just died. If I hadn't run into him at the bank, I never would have been paid because of the way his estate was managed.

— B.C. Ahouse

#173 – Thursday December 21, 2000

I met Paul Mellow at his farmhouse in Virginia through Bob Acun, who delivered hay from us to Paul. Mr. Mellow showed me around his immaculate premises, reminiscing about the hall he had built for his daughter's wedding to the fellow who later became a Virginia senator. These he'd demolished. Because of criticism of him being extravagant, he paid to have a church built on Route 50 between Middleburg and Winchester by medieval construction plans and methods. He also told me of a Rembrandt painting he bought and gave to the Smithsonian in D.C. I took my family to see it, and by then they had discovered a second portrait in the rear. It was painted on a board. In wandering around, I noticed a portrait of Picasso's sister by Picasso. When I touched it, it came off the wall. I called a guard and said to him somebody could steal this. He said, "Go ahead, I'll turn my back." I put it back on the wall.

—B.C. Ahouse

#174 – Thursday December 21, 2000

I met Mrs. Irene Dupont through Bob Craun, the occasion being Bob asking me to move a stone chimney that was to be used to build another on a home Irene was building for a son of hers. When we came together, Irene was chastising her son for having another child. It seems that for each new Dupont, a million dollars was immediately put in trust for the child, Irene's point being that her son was trying to break the family. Anyway, the old chimney was still standing and Irene, priding herself in explosives, had Bob back his lowboy trailer up to the chimney. Mr. Dupont said he could place the charge and drop it on the trailer. He did, but in doing so, he completely flattened the trailer. On the way out, we stopped at the Duponts' home and Bob asked Mrs. Dupont if she had a spare pack of cigarettes. She said sure, gave them to Bob and said 35 cents please.

— B.C. Ahouse

#175 – Thursday December 21, 2000

I always harbored some desire to have a dairy, and after my brother Alfred moved in with us — he needing a home and I needing a partner in the dairy — we, Irene and I, mortgaged the farm to Equitable Life Ass. Society, built a silo, and started the dairy business — both in cattle and buildings, and machinery. We made fair progress, but finances became trying after President Eisenhower removed milk support and our price dropped to $3.00 per hundred. The clincher in the matter was Polly-O Milk Products, who bought our milk. When I first met Mr. Polly-O, he came to me saying he needed three farmers to sign up. He had Bill Wagner and Carl Staffenker. He said, "Bernie, let me show you what I can do for you." When things got tough there was a meeting called at the American Legion in Interlaken. Mr. Polly-O said he had to be paid for hauling our milk.

I said, "Fellow, let's form a group to discuss this."

Polly-O said to me, "You S.O.B. you should be glad I buy your milk."

— B.C. Ahouse

#176 – Friday December 22, 2000

About ten years ago, I received a call from Roger Latto, an associate in the gas and oil business. Roger was with Great Lakes Holding located in Vancouver and Calgary. Roger said they had to sell their lease holdings in the U.S., and did I have any ideas? I said, "Sure, when do you want to sell them?" He said yesterday. I asked what was in it for us. He said the best he ever heard of was 33%. We verbally agreed. I called Bill Hoppa of Mitchell Energy in Columbus, Ohio and without much detail made a deal and planned to meet in Columbus. Roger flew to Toronto and then chartered a light plane to Columbus. My partner, Chuck Lucido, handled the details. He told Bill Hoppa to cut our check first. When Bill heard one third, he protested because of its excessive nature. Roger cut him off saying that's what we agreed to so cut the check. He did and everyone was satisfied. I should check on that amount with Chuck.

—B.C. Ahouse

#177 – Friday December 22, 2000

About 11 or 12 years ago, I received a phone call from Janet Reno, State Attorney 11th Judicial Circuit of Florida. I was asked if I knew a Frank Miller. I said yes, one in Florida. I was asked if I recalled staying with him a few years ago when I mentioned hearing a shot at night. I had no idea what this was leading up to. I said yes and was shortly subpoenaed to appear as a witness in the State of Florida v. Joyce Cohen. I knew nothing of this matter. They offered to pay my way to Miami, but I said I wouldn't go. Reno said they could send the marshals for me. I had made their acquaintance during the war and wouldn't go anywhere with them. It was then agreed that they would come to NY, which they did. Curiously, their recording equipment was stolen at the airport. They rented more in Syracuse and I have a videotape of the deposition and a printed copy of the same. Joyce Cohen was convicted. I feel very uncomfortable because of facts that came out in a book by a lady who sent me a copy. The defense lawyer did a poor job. I have other matters also.

— B.C. Ahouse

#178 – Friday December 22, 2000

I was often asked why I never ran for a public office and avoided the matter by saying it didn't interest me. I was elected to the NYS Conservation Department Association, but without my knowledge. A group of ladies in Albany asked me if there wasn't any job I'd like. I said sure, the U.S. Senate, explaining that I saw how exclusive their club was when I was around Washington, D.C. I was asked how I felt I could beat Jacob Javetts. I knew he didn't have much time left, but I simply said to ask all who weren't Jews to vote for me. This news got back to Seneca County before I did, and the GOP Committee jumped down my throat, asking me who I thought I was, promoting myself. To me, it was a joke. Anyway, I was later invited to their county meeting at the Holiday Inn in Waterloo, NY, where they set me up with a young congressman from Long Island who aspired for the Senate. He asked my advice on verbally promoting himself. I recall mentioning that he better get his story straight. He left the field empty for Alfonse d'Amoto to step in. Governor Carey assured his election by stating that this post should be maintained for a Jewish person.

—B.C. Ahouse

#179 – Friday December 22, 2000

I had an old Army friend, Gersham "Sarge" Phillips of Benton, Arkansas who often fed me info about the political scene there. Winthrop Rockefeller was old hat; Sarge had a "cousin" query me about how we took care of his brother, Nelson Rockefeller, the ex-governor. I said, "What do you mean?"

He said, "Having those two hookers knock him off like they did."

I said, "Who had them do that?"

He said, "His brother, David Rockefeller.

I asked, "Why?"

He said, "Now he can't testify about his roll in carrying interest to a legal usurious note.

I said, "That's hard to believe."

He said, "Then why did they cremate Rocky before he got cold?"

Just in the past year or so I met a jurist from Flemington NY, Randy Brokaw, who I related this to while drunk. He promptly named the two hookers.

—B.C. Ahouse

#180 – Friday December 22, 2000

I mention this ditty that I overheard at a meeting I just happened to notice as I walked by. A fellow, Timothy Leary, was the speaker and was asked by one of the audience how he could justify his promiscuous behavior. As best as I can recall, his answer went like this. "When a charismatic person is cognizant of his mythic potency, he arouses the basic animal desire in the opposite sex, and he pays homage to it in a manner that is harmonious and appropriate at the time."

—B.C. Ahouse

#181 – Saturday December 23, 2000

While staying at the Salty Dog in Florida in 1980, we made friends with Alan and Ida Hayes, from Seaton, Devon, England. They owned a cafe and insisted that we should be their guests as soon as we could make it. (We never did.) Alan was an interior contractor and decorator and spent six months of a year in Saudi Arabia working on the oil-rich Sheiks mansions. He told of one time while traveling on a barren stretch of road in the desert, his car was hit by a Saudi national. Alan was arrested and charged; the Saudi wasn't. The reason being that Alan shouldn't have been in Arabia. One story he related to us was when a couple—his friends—got drunk in Devon at a party and were stopped by a bobby who gave them a breathalyzer test, which they failed. They protested, saying the test must be faulty, please check on the baby. They did and the baby failed too. They were excused. The man said to his wife that it was smart to give the kid a couple of shots.

—B.C. Ahouse

#182 – Saturday December 23, 2000

Donald Gust was my school friend from first grade in Washington through high school. We graduated in 1938. Don went to law school (GI Bill) and became a federal judge in Oklahoma and Kansas. I saw little of him over the years, but about 20 years ago we ran into each other near Times Square on Broadway in NYC. Irene was with me, and Don had a good-looking lady on his arm, which disturbed Irene. Don invited us to dinner but Irene declined because of the young lady. I had dinner with them, and Don explained that because of the overloaded court system in NYC, he was brought in to help on the matter. The young lady was his court stenographer. At dinner, Don confided in me about the many times my help and relationship to him affected his decision in resolving the matter at hand on his bench. We met at reunions several times. Don passed away, but wrote a lengthy letter which I hope to return to his sister Dottie.

—B.C. Ahouse

#183 – Tuesday December 26, 2000

George Brooks married my sister Ruth in the Lutheran church in New York. George was a computer whiz and some 40 years ago developed the drum-type computer while with IBM. IBM had their reservations about it and had George set up his own business as a mutual designer. In seeking a location, I had George meet with the town father in Cronks restaurant in Interlaken. The locals only agreed to help if they got 51% control. That was impossible, so George built Mutual Designs in Owego, NY, which developed into a huge IBM facility. An altercation with the Robinson family resulted in George being forced out of the business for five years. He moved to Walton, where he developed the automatic teller for banking. In 1970, he moved to Henrietta, NY and went to work for Burroughs, who kept him busy with chips till way past 75 years old. George told me early in 1999 when the Y2K problem was being talked about that it was a farce. He was right.

— B.C. Ahouse

#184 – Wednesday December 26, 2000

During the late 1970s and early 1980s, on occasion I met with Dr. Fred in the Taft Hotel in NYC, where we often stayed over night. On one occasion, Irene and I were enjoying a before-dinner martini when a fellow (a salesman) approached us and said since he was a celebrating he would like to buy us a drink. He sat down with us and ordered a round. We had a pleasant time discussing the current events and I eventually asked him what he was celebrating. Well, he said, it started with their dog dying. I expressed my regrets. He said, "Don't be sorry, I'm not." I asked what he was celebrating. He said, "After a year of cleaning, we finally got the hair out of the house."

—B. C. Ahouse

#185 – Wednesday December 27, 2000

My father, Bernard Ahouse, couldn't handle booze, which encouraged me to stay away from it. I had a friend named Chester of Nanticoke, PA, who on coming down Newport Mountain near Fairchild Pond on his motorcycle, slid on the wet ash-covered pavement, sitting down hard. He broke his back and was paralyzed from the waist down. Chet learned the tax trade, and I kept him busy with things to do. However, at times he became extremely depressed and suicidal. We on occasion plied him with whiskey until he passed out, and in our minds he was safe. Of course, we helped him empty the bottle. I recall having my very first schooner of beer with Raymond Kurtz on Plymouth Mountain. It cost five cents (1939) after World War II. I couldn't shake the dysentery that plagued me. My wife's stepfather, John Olson, suggested I try gin because of its berry content. It helped, and I still enjoy a nice martini.

—B.C. Ahouse

#186 – Friday December 29, 2000

About 15 years ago, Corning Glass started up a new refractory and it exploded. The demolishing crew was instructed to salvage nothing. However, someone got out with a platinum "electrode" which he sold to my then son-in-law, Don Warren, for $1000.00. Don asked me if I knew anyone in the precious metal business. I did through my brother Morgan. I contacted the man Morgan knew, and he said to saw a piece off the bar and sent it to him. This was done, but when he got the sample, he said it is only a tungsten bar slated with platinum and not worth much. Don returned it and demanded his $1000.00 back (he got it). Later, Morgan recalled making such a bar for corning, not understanding the change in specs. Possibly the different quality caused the explosion and the order to salvage nothing.

            —B.C. Ahouse

#187 – Sunday January 7, 2001

When my mother, Edith Ahouse, was in her early 20s, she worked as a waitress in Syracuse, NY. She related many events and bad situations regarding her time there, but the most impressive to me was her telling about the purity of Lake Onondaga water and her enjoying swimming in it. This was in stark comparison to the Susquehanna River of Wilkes Bare, which was foully polluted from mine waste and sewage at the time. Today the opposite is probably true. The Susquehanna is cleaned up, and Onondaga is in bad shape. Nanticoke Creek was called the bleach creek because of mine waste. Raw sewage also ran into the creek.

— B.C. Ahouse

#188 – Sunday January 7, 2001

About ten years ago, I made the formal acquaintance of Louis Ehren Krutz through Alan Morton, who at the time was financial editor of the *New York Post*. My associate Charles Lucedo and I met Louis in Nyack, NY after spending the night there. Our business discussion was in regards to real estate that never materialized. My point in making this *** is Louis relating to us the *** and *** he enjoyed from government bureaucrats and that on the average he owed them $5000.00 a month to get rid of this foolishness. Alan Morton is married to my wife's cousin Sally. This situation was later referred to me by *** .

—B.C. Ahouse

#189 – Sunday January 7, 2001

About 10 years ago, I flew into the Newark airport from down south and had to find a transfer to Syracuse, which turned out to be People's Express — a short-lived local airline. After much waiting, I finally got on board, which resulted in another wait while they fueled the airplane. In doing so, something was stuck or improperly closed and suddenly there was an eruption of fuel, which completely closed the airport. The pilot calmly said, "Would everyone please evacuate the plane." I stayed in the seat because no one could move in the aisle; thankfully everyone got off. I was directed to another airplane, whereupon a ticket collector with a credit card machine came through demanding another $10.00 from each passenger.

— B.C. Ahouse

#190 – Sunday January 7, 2001

About 20 years ago, I bought 1000 shares of Tobin Packing Company stock for about $10.00 per share, the purpose being to encourage fellow farmers to join me and try to take control of the company, which had problems but was profitable. I received a call from the CEO, who explained that he thought likewise with the purpose of gaining a position on the NYSE listing. I tried to cooperate with him, and it appeared that he had the deal made. However, he called me one morning saying he went to bed thinking he had but woke up to realize he hadn't.

—B.C. Ahouse

#191 – Wednesday January 10, 2001

I was asked to attend a meeting at Banker's Trust Co. on Park Avenue in NYC. The meeting appeared to be a grease job by Halco. It was necessary for them to add directions. No one appeared, so I asked my wife Irene to nominate me. She did with some prodding. I embarrassingly seconded myself. The effect of this was for them to adjourn the meeting. It was then I met R. Fred Feit and his friend, an attorney from Rochester. He voted for me, as did Fred. This progressed to a lawsuit by Dr. Benjamin Blackman from South Carolina, who was supported by Ronsoldt I believe. Dr. Blackman and Ronsoldt did not appear to be friendly to me.

—B.C. Ahouse

#192 – Thursday January 11, 2001

Without my knowledge, Dr. Benjamin Blackman took this matter to a friend. As I recall, Halco spent over $8.5 m on counseling fees that were paid to Halco Gov. *** also rounded $2.5m to bid, which was spent on counseling fees to Halco. Dr. Blackman withdrew as the complainant after he was accused of dealing in drugs from his dentist's office in South Carolina. I was asked to replace him, which I did, and was deposed in the NYC law offices of the defendant. I humorously described myself as a poet. I don't recall ever being in court regarding this. However, Bill *** had himself and me named as directors. I never attended a board meeting, and Bill told me I was lucky not to be exposed to the Mafia. *** stock was replaced for the stolen funds.

—B.C. Ahouse

#193 – Thursday January 11, 2001

About June 6, 1997, Irene fell in our living room and broke her left hip in the socket ball. The Seneca ambulance gave her a rough ride to Cayuga Medical Center ER in Ithaca. There a Dr. Bruce Green had her X-rayed and admitted her for surgery. He inserted a pin in the ball and secured it with a plate and three or four screws. However, his screws came out, causing Irene extreme pain. We returned to his off-campus office, where the X-rays showed the problem. While I was awaiting the verdict, Dr. Green came into my presence, picked up a phone and chewed out an electrical contractor for a job poorly done and demanded an adjustment in payment. (Was he trying to tell me what to do?) Dr. Green then wanted Irene to go to Syracuse for a hip replacement but she preferred a Dr. Hale of Ithaca, who had replaced her cousin *** hip a few years back. This Dr. Hale did.

– B.C. Ahouse

#194 – Thursday January 11, 2001

Dr. Hale removed the existing pin implanted by Dr. Bruce Green and replaced the hip with a metal ball. Dr. Hale said he removed only one pin, which had come out of the hip ball. Dr. Hale said he had never heard of it happening. After the hip operation, Irene's leg became badly infected and had to be operated on again. During this time, a Dr. Moses from Elmira appeared at an early morning time and scared Irene badly by telling her that her leg would probably have to be removed. He overcharged Medicare and I refused to pay, telling his office that his service was useless. Dr. Hale took me to the X-ray archive and asked for Irene's present X-rays. He was told that they were given to Dr. Green with Hale's permission. He said not so and asked me if I had done so. I said no. Dr. Green's actions were questionable.

—B.C. Ahouse

#195 – Friday January 12, 2001

During 1944-1945, while I was at Remington Rand Propeller Division DPC in Johnson City, I had a fellow, apparently a Greek, who I was told to keep an eye on. He was missing for a few days once, and on his return he told me that he was in Montrose, PA when his car broke a rear axle. He walked to town, got a new one and replaced it himself on the road. About 20 years ago, several old acquaintances, George DeMopoles and Jim, whose last name I don't recall, and I were traveling, and since they were all Greeks, I related this story to them. They immediately thanked me for being a friend to George. He was supposedly a famous patriot from Cyprus, and they knew he had been here then.

— B.C. Ahouse

#196 – Sunday January 14, 2001

When I was in Houston at the NACD convention in 1974, my cousin Luther Domain, a police officer of the city and some-time caretaker of the downtown jail, showed me around. We went to the restricted area of the training basin when I saw a wheat ferry loaded and ready to sail to the USSR. From what I saw of the quality, we were lucky to have gotten rid of it. I remarked to the man showing us around about the size and number of the rats I saw. I asked him if they kept any cats. He said it was useless since the rats ate the cats. We also visited a Western store where I bought a corduroy Western coat and a set of mounted long horns. When I went to pay for them, my payment was refused. I asked why and was told "You're with Luther."

—B.C. Ahouse

#197 – Sunday January 14, 2001

Luther Domain also took me into the River Road Club, an exclusive abode of the wealthy. It was there that I made the acquaintance of Racehorse Harris and Joe Jameil, two prominent attorneys. I later introduced Joe to Bill Auble, re his problems with Texas. I never heard of an outcome. This place was certainly equipped for the elite. The carpets were so plush you had to pick up your feet with each step to keep from tripping. I had to go to the men's room, which had a large knocker. I knocked, and an attendant opened the door and handed me a jigger of scotch. I looked at it. He said, "Not your drink?"

I said, "No, I prefer gin."

He threw the glass and contents in the waste basket and poured me a double shot of gin.

—B.C. Ahouse

#198 – Sunday January 14, 2001

In 1974, Irene and I went to Galveston, TX with Luther Domain and his wife Jewell. We spent some time visiting, including a ferryboat trip to an adjoining island. Luther and his wife left early, and Irene and I spent about a week roaming around. One memorable evening was at a pizza parlor we stopped at during happy hour. Drink was free and two for one, so we each had two then the bartender handed us two for one again (four martinis). We ordered a pizza, which was thick crust and heaped up with almost everything imaginable, including a thick topping of black olives. We had regrets in eating it all but believe it or not nary a burp from it. Someone treated us to the pizza. What a night!

—B.C. Ahouse

#199 – Sunday January 14, 2001

In 1974, while Irene and I were in Galveston, we went for dinner in a large restaurant on the west side of town. We sat down near the window facing the gulf. There was another couple on the far side of the dining area. The gentleman came over, excused himself, and introduced himself and said it seemed foolish to stare at each other from long distance. Why didn't we enjoy dinner together? We did, and it was very interesting. They were from Iowa and were enjoying a seldom-taken vacation because his wife just had her first job termination at Tobin Packing in Iowa, where she was an executive secretary. It's not necessary to say I was delighted to hear her many versions of why Tobin was folding in Iowa. At the time, I was involved in a lawsuit with Halco and Tobin, mentioned in 190 and 191.

— B.C. Ahouse

#200 – Sunday January 14, 2001

The first time we drove through Texas going east, we drove into a Holiday Inn near Austin or San Antonio. Without knowing it, the main building was being remodeled, and we were put up in a trailer. The room was hardly bigger than a regular bath. If one stood up, the other had to lie down on the bed. There were no chairs. The water heater in the room was five gallons in size. We had checked in without knowing this and were stuck.

On a different trip, Luther Domain took us to visit a friend near the King Ranch. We were treated fine. The lady showed us around the cattle pasture, telling me to bring those two large buckets of rocks. I asked why. She said to throw at the mosquitoes. "If you don't hit them, I'd hold on to the other bucket and they won't carry you off."

— B.C. Ahouse

#201 – Tuesday January 16, 2001

When I was a teenager, I lived on West Washington Street, about a block from the Nanticoke State Hospital. My young brother Al, about six or seven years old, was admitted there with what was called the parrot's disease. His tongue swelled up to block off his mouth. Miraculously, he survived to this day. The hospital had an emergency admittance center to the right rear of the front. There was almost a constant flow of ambulances (which we called the Black Marias) from the numerous coalmines in the neighborhood. My friend John Brush (no relation) and I used to follow them in to see who was next and how badly injured they were. This came to an end for us when we saw John's father being brought in—he was dead.

— B.C. Ahouse

#202 – Tuesday January 16, 2001

About 30 years ago, I had some business with Si Diamond. He wasn't home, but his mother was there with a group of Jewish women who were chatting about their support of Israel. I quietly joined in their discussions, but when they asked me to support their efforts, I declined. I said I had no problems with the Hebrews wanting their own nation, but that I thought their location was a failing. They protested my belief but asked if I had some better idea. Since I didn't think that .01% of the world's people should jeopardize it (the world), I said they should locate in a more peaceful area. I suggested that Saudi Arabia (being very rich) could buy the Baja Peninsula from Mexico, which was in a sad financial state, and Israel should relocate there. They wouldn't hear of this, saying Moses had led them to their Promised Land. I remarked that Moses wasn't too clever, since he took them to the only place in the Middle East without oil. It seems that to date, the matter of location has only worsened.

— B.C. Ahouse

#203 – Tuesday January 16, 2001

Much ado has been made about the danger of a loaded gun in a car. But there is also a danger of one carelessly unloading a weapon. Some simply pump the magazine empty and after don't notice a shell still in the gun. One incident I can never forget happened in New Albany, probably in 1940. My cousin Fred MacLaughlin was pumping his rifle out when it accidentally fired. Our host, Judd Decker, was standing inches from the muzzle when it went off, missing him by inches. Poor Judd couldn't talk for the rest of the day.

On another occasion, my brother Alfred was loading my .22 Winchester pump rifle when it went off, discharging a bullet within a foot of my head. Howard Naugle, Uncle Leo Burman's brother-in-law, also contributed to these memories.

— B.C. Ahouse

#204 – Tuesday January 16, 2001

About 30 or 40 years ago, I was combing oats for Gerwin Schaeffer when I caught a fawn in the reel. I quickly shut the machine off and the animal was unhurt. I got down to extract the fawn. Its mother, a large doe, chased me and followed me up onto the combine. Another time I had the same experience, but I waited until I was sure the doe was not nearby. I got the fawn, a male, and put him over the fence into the woods. I notched his ear. Three years later, I shot a large buck within 50 feet of where I put him in the woods. His ear was notched. His head now hangs in my living room. Another time a doe with her gangrene front leg was stuck in a snow bank along Lodi Center Road. I squeezed the matter out of her left after I cut the foot off and tied it up with my shoelace. With three legs, I noticed her often. One year she bore three fawns. Another buck I took had a broken rear leg that had mended with the femur overlapping about four inches. It was completely welded together by bone. One hind leg was six inches shorter than the other.

— B.C. Ahouse

#205 – Tuesday January 16, 2001

I want to mention Bill Chamberlain, who was a fine man. He had a fine family, was a fine dairy farmer, restauranteur, state and national conservation director, and a benefit to everything he did. However, when the agricultural economy went sour in the 1980s, none of this mattered to the narrow-minded bank managers. As far as I know, they crucified Bill and he lost almost everything. I am not entirely sure of this or what became of Bill. However, the treatment of farmers was horrible—I myself included. Memories are why I support James Robertson of Jackson, Mississippi in his lawsuit against the Department of Agriculture.

—B.C. Ahouse

#206 – Wednesday January 17, 2001

I have known Bill Wagner for over 50 years and have had many experiences with him. Bill is the founder and owner of Wagner's Winery in Lodi, New York. Bill and I started farming in Lodi after WWII at about the same time. We both tried dairy farming and grain and seed farming. Bill had grapes and fruit. I had chickens. Fifty years ago, Bill wouldn't take a drink. I recall his saying beer was mule piss. Anyway, times change and Bill became fond of wine, since it was his own. I compliment him on his ambition and foresight. Recently he added micro-brewing to his itinerary, which prompted me to remind him of his prior appraisal of beer. He quickly said, "Compared to my brew, most beer is still like mule piss." Bill's Jenny Lee Café is another successfully endeavor.

— B.C. Ahouse

#207 – Wednesday January 17, 2001

A friend (of my father, Bernard Ahouse Sr.) named *** Weiss had a meat market on the public square in Nanticoke, PA. During the 1930s, we often got together as two families. Weiss had two sons, Harry and Alfred, who graduated with me from Nanticoke High School in 1938. He also had an older son who was going to medical school in Scotland. Not being knowledgeable about all these things, I asked him why go all the way to Scotland? He plainly told me that Jews were very limited in U.S. medical school admissions. I asked why. He replied that there was a real fear that if the Jewish doctors became too numerous, they would take over the medical profession. Whether or not that *was* so, it has apparently come to *be* so.

— B.C. Ahouse

#208 Thursday January 18, 2001

As a confessed pragmatic altruist, I feel obliged to correct the current fallacy of the social consequences as presented to the public regarding abortion. It is true that pro-choice is an option. However, it is a option that a person has to select in regards to their determination as to whether to endure an abortion or not. The two choices therefore are, shall I be pro-life or pro-death? This is how it should be addressed. Also on this matter, all births, marriages, divorces, or deaths are dutifully reported by our press. Wouldn't it also be proper for all abortions to be so recorded, especially those done at public expense? I ask this with the supposition that the public, liberal in general, would want to be free and open about these actions.

—B.C. Ahouse

#209 – Friday January 19, 2001

In June 1938, my brother Morgan and his friend Stanley Davilovich were working at the Admiral Hotel in Cape May, New Jersey. I was invited down to work as a painter. My mother's cousin Carl Dimich lived in Philadelphia, and he invited me to ride that far with him. In the meantime, his two nieces, Dorothy and Nancy, decided to go also, which put me in the rumble seat with his little son Carl Jr., who was about seven years old. The ride was tolerable until we got into the Poconos, where the cold air prompted me to lower the rumble seat cover, which slammed shut. Any pounding I did made no difference to Carl Sr., who was involved talking to the girls. The situation turned sour when Carl Jr. vomited, which after a while nauseated me too. Finally, we came to a halt and Carl Sr. opened the trunk. I popped up and vomited a lot in front of a church full of people that had just came out onto the street.

— B.C. Ahouse

#210 – Saturday January 20, 2001

Well, I finally made it to Cape May. I got the job at the Admiral Hotel as a painter, but they had no paint. So, I took a job in the kitchen and ran a large tunnel type dishwasher. But after a week, they had no money to pay me. I made the acquaintance of a fellow, Billy Knowles Knewel, who showed me around town and to his relatives' farm on the coast. The fishy taste of their milk was solved when I saw their cow eating dried fish along the beach pasture. I experienced my first taste of racial prejudice when a couple of men belabored me for being with a Cuban cook, a John Govin, who called me "bono chico." I just stayed away from him after that. I also learned how to deal cards in Pinochle one by one, not four in a hand as down in Pennsylvania by threat from a fellow who just returned from the Army in Panama. Old *** were going *** for a few thousand dollars.

—B.C. Ahouse

#211 – Saturday January 20, 2001

I often said that I grew up on the railroad. At least in 1940 I learned what hard physical labor was. Although I had worked on a temporary basis since 1936, I never had to keep up with a gang of Gandy dancers. By noon, I thought my back would break. But since it was the only job available, I held out and toughened up. Later, in the Army, men who thought I was a Brooklyn boy couldn't understand my physical strength and endurance. I became expert with a spiking hammer. I recall one time the foreman said, "Bernie, you've been spiking all day, take a rest – shovel for a while." Rail over ten meters long, the gauge was four feet eight and a half inches—a chalk line from the length of two rails measured in the center—six inches gave you a six degree curve. Track level by notches gave you the pitch of the curve. Three blocks of wood, one with a peep sight, gave you a leveling length tool. All you needed to build a railroad. Nanticoke Brand New Jersey Central Railroad.

—B.C. Ahouse

#212 – Friday January 26, 2001

A few years ago, while in Atlantic City with Irene, I met his Joe Brieker's fiancée, Francine Covin. While sitting alone with Covin, she asked me pointedly if there was a possibility of rape in a marriage. I said that was a possibility, but if she wanted to entertain that situation, she should also consider the possibility of prostitution, which opened up the matter of what should be expected of each other. I said that to satisfy other needs, the matter of cheating arose as most often applied to the male. He is cheating on his wife if he does not satisfy her and then forsakes her for another. Cheating on the part of the female could be with another person or maybe denying him of his needs or cheating him out of his expectations.

— B.C. Ahouse

#213 – Friday January 26, 2001

I want to recall a job Irene's Uncle Fred Asay Sr. did for us (no charge) when we moved into our present home in March 1946. Fred dug a ditch by hand about a hundred feet long to a modest depth of two feet. He hand laid one-foot-four-inch-long tile with a half-inch gap between them, covering each opening with a heavy cover of asphalt roofing. Fred said we would never have any trouble with the drain since the varmints, moles and snails would keep it open. I often bragged about this, and we never had any problem whatsoever until last fall when a drainage problem developed. I thought I had remedied it several times, but right after Christmas it plugged tight. Carl Van Vleet days up the line east of the house and it took water freely – it was plugged up the 1 ½ lead pipe under the porch which he flushed out with his cone-like device and water pressure. Probably plugged by one of those varmints, but not a
***

— B.C. Ahouse

#214 – Sunday January 28, 2000

When Nelson Rockefeller was governor of New York, he proposed increasing state salaries to commercial levels to attract better people. This he did, but I don't know if he got better people. My idea of them have a union (CSEA) gave them the best of two worlds, especially the 20-year retirement. Their political clout as a group was also immensely increased. When I was on the State Board (NYSCD), I made a token motion to consider making dairy farmers eligible for a 20-year pension. This was shot down because of the expense and that they were not state employees. My response was "whatever," they are still the most important people working in the state and should be given the same entitlement.

— B.C. Ahouse

#215 – Monday January 29, 2001

Need Help on This One…much left out and unable to read.

1. I became acquainted with William "Bill" Pousoldt during the Tobin Packing fiasco and stuck with him through the legal proceedings, which cost me 1000 shares and Tobin $10,000, Bill advised me to refer to ourselves as "Associates." Which I never did.

2. The last deal I worked on for him was with JC Penney Inc. Plans taxes which never materialized. To Pousoldt's disgust, I never learned the intricacies of its finality.

3. A matter in 1993 requiring the Elcapitan Ranch in Santa Barbara. I did his bidding in discussions with Texaco Exxon – Trust for public land – Rockwell Bullard III never received notice of any settlement with Texaco or others.

—B.C. Ahouse

#216 – Friday February 2, 2001

I met Tony Taonuro some 30 or 40 years ago when the Fish and Wildlife people sent him here to appraise the potential wildlife ponds and marshes, which didn't get done. When I was on the State Board (NYSCD), I met him in NYC when he was in charge of pollution control in Long Island Sound. I asked if he could clean it up. He said not unless we got rid of the dog feces in the western end. Having noticed the horrible contamination on the city sidewalks, I suggested that the dog owners should bear their responsibility and clean it up. Our efforts resulted in help from the Pooper Scooper scheme. Incidentally, Tony told me that his negative Wasserman test was not caused by syphilis but by a dog disease he'd picked up as a child.

—B.C. Ahouse

#217 – Saturday February 3, 2001

When we started to farm here in 1946, we took the advice of the extension agent from Seneca Co. and Cornell. The one thing that bothers me is their advice, almost demand, to treat our oat seed with cerasin to prevent *** on the grain. It worked quite well, but it was a mercury compound and we had no idea of its potential danger until years later. As directed, we spread it on the seed and turned it over manually with scoop shovels until all were colored pink, like was the chemical. The lasting effect of it was for us to pass gas for several days that smelled like cerasin. I, on occasion, asked if any research was done on this, but I never got an answer.

—B.C. Ahouse

#218 – Tuesday February 6, 2001

Most of my family and friends are well acquainted with and own firearms. There have been a few accidents that I am aware of. About 50 years ago, my cousin Herbert Sutken was shot in the leg by my Uncle Richard Burman when he was cleaning a .22 rifle in my grandmother's room. Some years later, my neighbor and friend was shot in the leg by a stray bullet from a .22 rifle when my brother Morgan and Anthony Kotalak were target shooting in Tony's basement. The bullet ricocheted out a window and hit him. A cousin of my Uncle Fred MacLaughlin was shot in the arm and side by a shotgun blast of buckshot when shooting pumpkins they were throwing in the air. This happened on the River Fluss at Nanticoke.

—B.C. Ahouse

#219 – Tuesday February 6, 2001

I have a Winchester Model 06 .22 pump rifle serial #627132 which I bought when I was 10 or 12 years old for only $2.00. I earned the money cleaning out the ovens for a baker on Hanover Street in Nanticoke. The seller was waiting for me, and it was hard to part with my first two bucks. Anyway, probably 16 years later I loaned the gun to my close friend Stanley A. to go squirrel hunting. He ended up on the north side of Nuangola Lake and decided to take a shortcut across the lake. When crossing the lake's outlet, the ice gave way and Stanley fell into the water. He threw the rifle ahead of him onto the ice. Luckily, he got out and started back home. When he was on top of the Seward Mountain going to Nanticoke, he remembered the gun, and though soaked and frozen he retraced his steps and retrieved my .22 rifle—I still have it on the wall in my office.

—B.C. Ahouse

#220 – Tuesday February 6, 2001

Back when we were shipping a lot of hay, one of our truckers was Sam Juriger from the Binghamton area. He handled a lot of hay to the Binghamton Zoo. The person I became acquainted with there was named Clarence. I never knew his last name. Sam often mentioned him and his activities. After a spell of not hearing Clarence mentioned, I asked Sam how he was. Well, Sam said he got a little careless cleaning up the lions' pen and the sorry fact was that they ate him. That really is what happened to Clarence.

— B.C. Ahouse

#221 – Wednesday February 7, 2001

One of the truckers from the Lancaster, PA area was Irvin Reed, who was quite responsible but occasionally short of money. After loading two of his trucks, they being driven by his sons, he called me at suppertime and asked me to go to Watkins Glen Sheriff and pay their traffic fines of $300.00 for both. I don't know what their ticket was for. This I did on the promise of quick repayment, which never happened. Later I stopped at his home in PA and he humbly apologized and explained his cash shortage problem. His wife was a compulsive shopper who bought many objects but never even opened the packages. His two-car garage was full of them. Some years later, he sent a friend here for hay who paid me $100.00 on the account — that was it. I think Irvin had a stroke and died.

—B.C. Ahouse

#222 – Wednesday February 7, 2001

Amos Rhet was an Amish friend of Irvin Ree who left the church, bought a truck, and went into the hay business. He told me his father wouldn't sit down to watch his TV, but he would stand in the doorway with head half turned. Amos was always short of money and once gave me a check which he said was good. It bounced. He said he would make it good or his father would. This never happened, and after much dialogue, I turned it over to the sheriff for collections in Seneca County. I had to go to the grand jury (only once for me). He was indicted and after much promising, he never made it good. But with threats from the sheriff, his father did. I never saw Amos again.

—B.C. Ahouse

#223 – Tuesday February 13, 2001

In March 1995, shortly after Irene left the Geneva Hospital, and we sold most of our land to the Trust for Public Land, who immediately sold it to the federal government, two men, a Mark something and a deputy sheriff, came to my office door. I politely welcomed them in. Mark at once began shouting in a loud voice to get out immediately. Irene, who was in bed at the other end of the house, was scared to death. I demanded to know what they were talking about. They left at once. Some time later, Brayton Foster, supervisor of Covert, stopped me on the street in Trumansburg, mentioned this incident, and asked if I knew why the sheriff was there. I said not really. Brayton said they hoped I'd get violent so they could arrest me.

                                                          — B.C. Ahouse

#224 – Tuesday February 13, 2001

During 1976, while at the NACD Convention in Honolulu, some of my friends from Oklahoma – Fred *** , Bud Tucker, and *** Hi *** were discussing going to Australia to inspect a ranch. They invited me to go along, but I begged off as a poor boy. They laughed and needled me about being a big landowner in NY. I said, "Yeah, but I don't own any oil wells." They offered to pay my way, but I declined but said, "Why don't you develop the gas and oil on my NY land?" A few months later, a Leon Scully showed up. He paid me $1,000.00 to help him start a lease program. This led to my meeting Chuck Lucido and my relationship with him that was profitable, and to this day we are friends.

— B.C. Ahouse

#225 – Friday February 16, 2001

Before there was any known or publicized dope problem in our South Seneca school districts, some sage made up his mind to get a supposed reformed addict to lecture the local students on drug abuse. Shortly after, the problem began to raise its ugly head in our area. It became obvious that my nephew, David Ahouse, Al's son, was well aware of this. I asked him what prompted him to experiment. He simply said that this lecture aroused his and other's curiosity, and they decided to be cool. To me this lecture opened the doors on this evil.

— B.C. Ahouse

#226 – Saturday February 17, 2001

I have previously commented on the unfairness of less than a tenth of 1% of the world's population jeopardizing the whole. In fact, how can the Jews, who are a religious group, be so highly subsidized by the U.S. government? Also, how can so small a group, regardless of their financial finesse, feel justified in doing so? So as not to stand here alone, and I mean no malice to the Jews, I only plead that this mess be resolved.

—B.C. Ahouse

#227 – Saturday February 17, 2002

In the summer of 1941, Irene and I, while we were single, went to Atlantic City in my 1937 Ford V8 two-door with my sister Ruth and her friend Moe, who worked for the Susquehanna Coal Company in Southern Luzerne County, PA. We made the rounds in AC, it being the first time there for all of us. We still have a photo of Irene and I strolling down the boardwalk. This was before anybody ever heard of a pizza. On our way home, while going through Trenton, New Jersey, we were stopped by some local folks who were vending what they called tomato pies. They cost 25 cents a piece, and they were filling and delicious. I believe this is where pizzerias got started. In Binghamton, NY, they still call pizzas by their original name, tomato pies.

— B.C. Ahouse

#228 – Monday February 19, 2001

Throughout the years, I employed many men and boys on the farm here in Lodi. The fellows always kept their own time, and I never questioned it unless it looked too out of line. The workweek ended on Friday night, and I always paid them on Saturday. On one occasion, about 15 or so years ago, Thomas Furr worked on Saturday only and asked for his pay. I explained the system. He left but later his grandmother, Gertrude Furr, brought him out and glaringly asked for his pay. To avoid a controversy, I paid him his few bucks. This supplied his beer money at the Lodi bar. He got drunk with a Jennings boy, took George Jennings' car, and started east on 96A. He hit a car full of a family and as I recall killed four people. Did my breaking my pay system result in this?

—B.C. Ahouse

#229 – Monday February 19, 2001

While I was stationed at Ft. Belvoir, VA in 1942-43, I usually tried to associate with any newcomers, especially if they seemed alone or aloof. At one time, there were several fellows in a neighboring company who seemed to be keeping to themselves. At first, they didn't respond to my approach but finally began to associate with me. They were really stout and tall men. They chose to be called the range people and were from Texas. In time, it turned out that they were Comanche Indians. Once, I told them that there were some Sioux from the Dakotas in a company close by, and I would like to get them all acquainted. I was soundly deflated when I was told that they wanted nothing to do with those damned Yankees.

— B.C. Ahouse

#230 – Monday February 19, 2001

Since everything should contain a little humor, I again insert a little short story or joke. This fellow who always had a hard time adjusting to anything or everything moved into a section of town which was predominantly an Italian neighborhood. After trying all of his feeble efforts in associating with his group, he made the remark that he really owed his life to a group of Italians. Asked how, he said that they saved his life during the war by hiding him in their attic. He was asked if this happened in Naples. After a deep breath he slowly said no, it was in South Philadelphia during WWII.

—B.C. Ahouse

#231 – Wednesday February 21, 2001

One morning in the 1970s, I was deer hunting on Hatch Mt., PA, where we had a cabin and a trailer. Upon one mountain, I shot an eight-point buck at the break of dawn, just before it began to rain hard. The carcass practically floated down the log road. When I got to Clarence Hatch's cabin, he invited me in for breakfast. I accepted his offer and hung the deer up in a tree on his property. While I was enjoying Clarence's pancakes and sausage, someone began yelling, "Ahouse, come out so I can arrest you." A PA game warden was standing in the pouring rain and accused me of violating the law by not being on Hatch's hunting roster. I told him I was on my own down the road and to get lost. As I wouldn't cooperate with his folly, he returned with his captain and a PA state trooper. I explained my position to the captain. He said it was proper. The game warden became mad and very adamant. The captain and trooper had to force him into the car to leave. End of threat.

— B.C. Ahouse

#232 – Wednesday February 21, 2001

Another Pennsylvania hunting story worth telling involves a friend, "Skip" Hatch, who was the grandson of Clarence Hatch, our camp neighbor. Skip used to hunt mornings only because of his night job at Ingersoll Rand in, I believe, *** . His grandmother always asked him how luck was on his return home. He once jokingly told her, "Yeah, I got a nice buck but just when I got through gutting him, he got up and staggered down the hall where a fellow from Philadelphia shot and claimed him." His grandmother thoroughly believed this to be true and called the story into the Towanda newspaper, which printed it as a fact. It must have been believed because it made it into the national wire and was reprinted throughout the country. It was a complete fabrication.

— B.C. Ahouse

#233 – Thursday February 22, 2001

One morning about 30 years ago, either Tim or Tom Morrow (twins), who were my brother Al's in-laws, came running up to my house screaming to please come down to Al's to do something. I ran down the distance of about 500 feet, went into the house and found Al traumatized. His year-old daughter Melanie was sitting on the living room floor crying, and his wife Barbara was comatose on the floor and turning blue. Because of domestic problems, something had turned matters for the worse—Barbara had overdosed. My thoughts were on what to do, and if I should do anything. The little baby crying decided that for me. I turned Barbara on her side to clear her mouth, applied body pressure and breathed into her mouth. Not soon, but she showed some improvement by the time the medics got there. Their remark was there wasn't much they could accomplish in doing anything. I kept working and they did also. Well, needless to say, Barbara survived. My words to Al were, "You're overreacting," which he threw back to me years later.

—B.C. Ahouse

#234 – Thursday February 22, 2001

About 20 some year ago, Irene and I were visiting her sister Peggy Seely's family in Delancey, NY. I wandered out to the rear of their residence, where their son Danny (who is now a Ph.D. teaching in Michigan) was in the process of building a tree house in a branch about 20 feet above the ground. In watching what he was doing, I felt almost compelled to ask him to come down. Before I could say anything, the worst happened. Some of his footing broke loose and Danny was thrown to the ground, landing flat on his back. I immediately went to him, straightened out his body and started to breathe air into his lungs. Peggy and Irene came up. I kept working on Danny and told them to get a doctor. Peggy was distraught, but her husband Tom appeared nonchalant—not realizing what had happened. Luckily though, no bones were broken and Danny recovered fully.

—B.C. Ahouse

#235 – Friday February 23, 2001

The recent death of Dale Earnhardt brings to mind my first introduction to stock car racing. Two good farmers, Gordan Herryman and Bryon Harris, who also ran a ditching business whereby I made their acquaintance, somehow were enticed to support a racing group of locals, and they invited me to participate. I declined. Not too much later at the Waterloo fairgrounds, there was a serious accident. A stock car landed on Gordon and Byron was hit in the high back by a tire and wheel and was presumed dead. Both were hospitalized. Byron survives to this day. Gordon's recovery was slow and painful. He made a special trip out here to my home to tell me that I was wise to stay out of the dumb business and keep away, and that he wishes that he had also. He died a short time later. His farm was sold off after his son was advised by Cornell faculty to forget about the farm since farming is seldom profitable.

— B.C. Ahouse

#236 – Friday February 23, 2001

In December 1994, while my wife Irene was in intensive care at Geneva General Hospital in terrible shape with not much hope of survival, a Catholic priest, who was called Father Mike, while making his rounds approached me and commented about Irene. He asked if we were Catholic. I said no, but we are Christians. He offered his prayers, I accepted, and together he and I recited the Lord's Prayer. Irene was not aware of this, but I believe she felt its influence. I gave my thanks and wished him well. The terrible end of this brief acquaintance was when I read in the *Finger Lakes Times* of Father Mike being killed late at night around Christmas. He fell asleep while driving to Corning, NY to visit his mother. He hit the broad steel guardrail which broke and came into the car, killing him outright.

—B.C. Ahouse

#237 – Tuesday February 27, 2001

About 35 years ago on a pleasant summer afternoon, my daughter and her girlfriends were swimming in our pond on the north side of Smith Road. The girls in their swimsuits provided a distraction for a college professor from Auburn who was married to our neighbor's daughter, Pricilla Hatch (I don't recall his name). Jan Shoebride, a toddler of two or three years of age, was on the swing in our yard and she suddenly decided to cross the road. In a flash, she was on the road and was hit by the professor's car. I ran to her. Her leg was askew of her body. I tried to rearrange her body, and I held her close. Susan ran for her father, and I gave Jan to him. The professor said, "What did you expect me to do, go into the ditch?" This angered Susan, who began hitting him and screaming at him. I took her arm and said not to make things worse. At this point, Pooch, our dog, nailed my leg; it was the first time a dog bit me. Thankfully, Jan recovered.

—B.C. Ahouse

#238 – Wednesday February 28, 2001

Around the late 1970s early 1980s, Congress passed a Clean Water Act. One provision of it was section 208 on non-point pollution, which was to control any pollution not coming out of a tack or pipe. Governor Carey of New York appointed a Hank Stebens to implement the rules and regulations. The State Conservation District Board directed me to work with and cooperate with Stebens to get this done. Stebens was very arbitrary about this and wanted one set of railroads for the entire state. Since conditions varied, I wanted each geological area approached properly. He wouldn't have it. Thinking that no one would be there, he called the first hearing in Manhattan. A sizable crowd attended and would approve his method. He thought no attendance would enable him to avoid the next four meetings. They were never held to my recollection, and to this date he believes we have no R+R.

— B.C. Ahouse

#239 – Wednesday February 28, 2001

Back about 1980, Chuck Lucido and I were obtaining gas leases in North Carolina, working with three men from Burnsville, NC. One incident that remains in my mind is the fellow at the firehouse in Buladean bragging about their lynching the last black man in the South. It seems that he was seen on the other side of a fast-moving stream, alone, along the main road on top of a young girl. They assumed he was trying to rape her. I asked if he possibly had pulled her out of the creek and was trying to revive her. No response to my question. Another interesting matter was the Register of Deeds in Avery County asking me to bear with her since several *** had burned down the courthouse in 1860s and they hadn't got the records back in shape yet. Another incident was the social undertakers throwing the drained blood of a corpse into a road ditch adjoining his business.

—B.C. Ahouse

#240 – Thursday March 1, 2001

My first recollection of Jim Van Vleet, the son of Stanley and Mary, was when I was doing the installation of a new hot water heating plant on their home on Route 414 in Lodi, NY. I had just returned back from lunch at home and gone upstairs to work. Jim was about 14 and tearfully said, "Get me out of here, mister." We hunted and associated over the years. When I hung up the farm business, Jim bought my 403 1H combine at the sale, but later scrapped it, changing it for the 1440 1H, which was a better machine. Since he needed the shop and storage on CR. 137, I made him a deal at $25,000 with 6% interest. His comment was that it was the best financial deal anybody offered him. Jim also bought the shop tools for $1,000.00 cash. I mention all of this just because of the fact that Jim was the most honorable man I ever dealt with in the sale of many items over the years. I admire his determination to make a go at organized farming, a tough man.

—B.C. Ahouse

#241 – Friday March 2, 2001

With all the current discussion over the failings of our public schools, I would like to state again my own opinion. I firmly believe that the teacher should intelligently focus on teaching what is required for the first three days of school. The fourth shall focus on review of what was taught and proper testing of all involved. On the fifth day the teacher would turn to helping those who were failing, and those who passed would be excused to pursue channels of their own choosing—sports and other topics—or be excused from school. As far as more money being the NEA president's excuse and demand, I recall in the late 1940s my schoolteacher friends Bob Jacopy, Ralph Whitehead, Jim VanGaled, SC Meyes, all needed more than their meager salary, which was better than the average income for like people. I asked how much? All they could say is more.

—B.C. Ahouse

#242 – Tuesday March 6, 2001

I first met Darell Travers when he was a school chum of my daughter Nancy. I recall that he made a present of some rabbits to her that she raised many from, eventually turning them loose in the nearby woods. As a young boy, Darrell worked here on the farm. On one occasion I left him in the barn to replace a battery in a tractor with instructions to bring it to the home place in the morning. He never showed up. When I looked for him, he was sitting on the tractor, saying it wouldn't start. I asked if he had checked the battery. He said it was gone. He denied any knowledge of what happened, so I called the state police, telling him to wait there. The trooper knew where to go and after questioning him came up and said, "The boy has your battery, should I charge and arrest him?"

I said, "No. Let me handle it." I told Darrell it was a foolish thing to do and not repeat such actions.

—B.C. Ahouse

#242B – Tuesday March 6, 2001

Darrell worked the summer, and after graduating from school, I believe he entered the military service. On returning home, he started farming on his own. The tragedy of it was that while turning a tractor to start it, it upset and killed his younger brother. He changed farms with a wife and lost the barn to the Electric Co. by fire. He sued NYSEG and collected. He then moved back to Lodi, started a new farm and began delivering several newspapers with employers. He somehow got convicted of molesting young girls and served some time in county jail. A few years later, he was charged again and in considering the eventual consequences, he shot himself to death on Butcher Hill.

— B.C. Ahouse

#243 – Tuesday March 6, 2001

While leasing gas and oil rights in the mountains of North Carolina and Tennessee, I met a very tall fellow called Hi Walker. I commented about his name, asking who gave it to him. Since he was about seven feet tall, he said his parent did. When he was born, his name was really Hiram. He offered to introduce me to a family of Martins in a remote area, with my promise that I wouldn't bother with their women or drink their whiskey. One parcel was originally the Iron Mountain Resort in the middle 1800s—the deed had been quietly claimed back and forth numerous times by a Deywoldes family. The gas and oil rights appeared to be neglected in the title and we took a lease from a family who claimed them. Shortly, we were visited by representatives of R.J.R. and simply told if we were injuring our health to forget about the lease.

—B.C. Ahouse

#244 – March 6, 2001 Tuesday

Although my wife Irene was always very concerned about what people's opinions of her were, and also some of my other family members, I honestly believe that I never much cared what anybody thought of me. Not that I felt superior, I just didn't let others' opinions bother me. For a long time though, I had what is called stage fright. I can't explain this, I just felt uncomfortable when vocally facing a crowd. Perhaps I didn't want to offend others with my remarks. I only mention this because I cannot explain it. In later years though, I outgrew this obsession. I chaired the Seneca County Conservation District for many years and sat as a director on the NYSCD Board without any of these ancient abnormal behaviors.

—B.C. Ahouse

#245 – Friday March 9, 2001

Two days ago, I went into the Citgo gas station in Interlaken to pay my bill. The little terrier dog as usual was sound asleep on the couch, being covered with a blanket with only his head showing. Without warning, he burst awake with a fury of barking. Larry Potts, the owner, said it was just a dog in the car that had just driven in. "He does that all the time when another dog shows up." The car's windows were closed, as was the station door. Larry asked me how he could so swiftly detect another dog. I was without a clue and am deeply puzzled as to the strange phenomenon that dogs possess.

— B.C. Ahouse

#246 – Wednesday March 14, 2001

I have noticed quite a lot of foolish actions by so-called police officers, but one of the most hilarious happened in Lake Worth, Florida about 20 years ago. My mother-in-law, Tillie Olson, lived on S. 10th Street and because of the suitability, she parked her car in front of her co-op apartment on the curb of the street. Late one night, the police were chasing a renegade who took a side street, lost control of his car, hit Tillie's car and drove it up onto the sidewalk in front of her house. To make something out of their efforts (I believe the guy got away), the cop wrote Tillie up for parking on the sidewalk. This infuriated her and she took it out on the police sergeant at his office, who to escape her wrath, canceled the ticket.

—B.C. Ahouse

#247 – Wednesday March 14, 2001

I spent much of my young life in Nanticoke, PA — 1927-1941. One of the circumstances that I must mention was my brother Alfred's relationship with Nick Adarinschik, who became Nick Adams when he went to Hollywood. He gained some fame, but died at age 36 from an overdose of prescription medicine. Another personality was Edie Adams, no relation to Nick. She was of German descent, and she and I were first acquainted as infants so my mother said. I knew her briefly as a teenager. She was a popular movie star. Also, a fellow who I only knew casually was Lee Tracey, also of Hollywood fame. Russ Morgan was a Nanticoke native and a friend of my mother Edith. While she was single, I knew her to see him on occasion.

— B.C. Ahouse

#248 – Wednesday March 14, 2001

While in the U.S. Army in 1942-1943 at a class of instructions about the war, I asked what the war was really about. The major simply said that it was about an ocean of oil in Arabia. The subject was about how to lessen or eliminate the threat of war that usually started in Europe. In my mind, I harbored the thought of making Europeans more acceptable to the world. No one seemed to be too enthralled by the French, Germans, or Italians. So, I suggested that all these join the Swiss Confederation, making most Europeans Swiss and more likely embraced. Seems like the EU is taking on the task now. As a post note, I never really admired the British Empire, but I acknowledge that nothing better has replaced it.

—B.C. Ahouse

#249 (These will be added later.)

#250

#251 – Thursday March 25, 2001

Back in the 1960s-1970s, I had several ridiculous relationships with the Marine Midland Bank in Elmira. I may have noted them previously. In any respect, the present head of the New York Banking Authority, Ms. Muriel Seibut contacted me, having got my name from the record. It seemed that the Hong Kong Shanghai Bank of Asia was preparing to take over the Marine Midland Bank, a New York State Institution, which she protested. I gave her all the information that I could, which was instrumental in killing the deal. Marine Midland then left the New York State Charter and became nationally affiliated, which allowed the merger to take place. I don't believe this helped New York any.

— B.C. Ahouse

#252 – Friday March 16, 2001

Before I was six years old, my father, Bowey, as he was called, often took me into a speakeasy run by Chucky Leski on the corner of Nobel and Prospect Streets in Nanticoke. This was across the street from Pulaski School, where I entered the 6th grade. When I was but six, I became adept and fascinated by a penny coin gambling device — this was a glass-fronted series from Paris with a hole in the opposite side. The challenge was to put a penny in the coin slot, hit the start hinge and drive it into the hole. Probably because it was eye level to me, I became very expert at winning. This was a talent when I was six, but when I was 12 going to school across the street, Chucky never let me near it. Coincidently, our Uncle Morgan Rees had one on his tobacco counter in his store on the park in Nanticoke. Much later in my teens, I and my brother Morgan remodeled the store. Uncle Morgan was there when we moved the counter to gather the trove of pennies that had fallen into a crack on the right side.

—B.C. Ahouse

#253 – Monday March 26, 2001

My first experience with a tragic death occurred when I was five or six years old. Two of our neighborhood children, a boy and a girl, were sled riding on the bank of the Susquehanna River in South Wilkes Barre. What happened was that the ice gave way and they disappeared under it. I was a part of the crowd that gathered, and to my knowledge, the bodies were not immediately recovered. Shortly afterward, the mother of my friend Bernard Livingston of Hargrove up and died of pneumonia. This was followed by the death of a family friend, Otto, of pneumonia and appendicitis. This all left a lasting impression on me.

— B.C. Ahouse

#254 – Monday March 26, 2001

Perhaps the behavior problems of our young children today could be partly improved by the institution of a curfew. When I was a young boy in Nanticoke, ours was strictly enforced by the city police. The number 7 Colliery of the Susquehanna Coal Company at 9:00 p.m. sharp sounded long blasts to declare the curfew. The officer who usually broke up the gang on W. Washington and Maple Streets was a short man by the name of Herman Lepke. If anyone didn't move when ordered to break it up, it ended with a short chase with the officer usually catching the culprit and delivering him home.

—B.C. Ahouse

#255 – Monday March 26, 2001

Because of the recurring bad spell my wife Irene had yesterday, I am prompted to refer to the dispatch Rochester Judge Patricia Marko decided regarding Irene's mutilated body. Judge Marko, who was a replacement for the original judge and a friend of the wife of the administrator of Geneva General Hospital, implied to our lawyer, Joanne Hart Piessrua that we had better accept the meager offer that was maneuvered by the insurance company and Joanne's partner, J. Harrell. I informed all involved that we were coerced into accepting the meager offer. My thought is what would either of these women want to be paid to have like damage done to their bodies?

— B.C. Ahouse

#256 – Monday March 26, 2001

I realize that it is of no great consequence, but I often recall that when I was in the Station Hospital (with pneumonia) at Fort Hamilton, Brooklyn, New York, the well-known prizefighter Sugar Ray Robinson was brought into the hospital for evaluation by a squad of MPs. The word passed around was that he refused to board a troop ship for overseas and became quite belligerent.Apparently, he didn't view the war as his fight, and he was quite amiable as far as I was concerned. Incidentally, some years later my brother Alfred Ahouse met him on a plane to California and spent a pleasant trip with him.

— B.C. Ahouse

#257 – Tuesday March 27, 2001

I wish to set down some of the loudest, and perhaps otherwise, memories of my daughter Susan from when she was a child. When she was about two, I was getting her ready for bed with a bath and clean pajamas. I had recently reupholstered a small settee. She wouldn't go to the bathroom but climbed up on the new furniture and really emptied her water on it. Her only remark was a big "See?" She got spanked.

Another time she showed her brother Karl a bag and said, "Candy." He chased her all over the yard, caught her on the porch and took the bag from her with its contents of stones.

Another time a pair of her panties blew off the line and froze solid on the lawn. On my way back to work, I said to her mother on the porch, "Catch!" They took off like a Frisbee and went through the kitchen window.

— B.C. Ahouse

#258 – Tuesday March 27, 2001

In all fairness, I should record some of the dumb things that we, or should I say I, did. During the tail end of WWII, most everything was scarce, including pillows. Our newborn son Karl rested well on ours, but it became saturated, so I decided to wash the feather pillow in a tub washing machine. It became a soaking mess which I tried to finish drying on the attic floor of 25 Dayton Street, Westover, NY. What a fluffy mess. Probably there are still some feathers there. When we came on the farm, one of the first things we attempted was to make maple syrup by boiling the sap down on our wood-fired kitchen stove. We didn't get much syrup, but we managed to steam all the wallpaper off the ceilings and walls.

—B.C. Ahouse

#259 – Thursday March 29, 2001

While I was in the Fort Belvoir Hospital in 1943, the fact that I was suffering from pneumonia was well documented, but the fact that I contracted malarial fever was not to my knowledge. I know it because the everlasting fever I suffered prompted me to go to the laboratory and ask for a blood test to identify the cause. Because of the prevalence of malaria there, the technician readily showed me a bluish bacteria on a sample of my blood. I promptly recalled a time during a routine blood test in Fort Belvoir where the medic used an old-fashioned pen point to puncture my finger for blood. He used the same point on a long line of men—some of whom had just returned from India, the home source of this malaria.

– B.C. Ahouse

#260 – Thursday March 29, 2001

Twenty years ago, when I was a director on NYS Area Fish and Wildlife Board in Avon, NY, I made the proposal to encourage and transplant the wild turkey. I relied on the hunting of these that I did in Pennsylvania and was aware of the remarkable recovery they had made from the 1930s. This was done partly by penning hens in the few areas that some wild ones still existed to be bred by wild toms. The biologist Larry McGus would not accept my suggestion, quoting that our area was too open. I replied by the mentioning the huge flocks I saw on the open prairies of Oklahoma. Regardless, the turkeys made their comeback by themselves. Last spring I counted 55 turkeys in the field adjoining my home in Lodi. I saw a hen yesterday.

— B.C. Ahouse

#261 – Thursday March 29, 2001

The first summer we were on the farm, in 1946, we had Nelt Rusbaugh's crew baling hay; My Buckrake used his stationary baler. It was long tedious work. As was the custom here at that time, we provided noontime dinner for all concerned. Our first daughter, Susan, was born July 6, 1946 at Seneca Falls Hospital, where Irene spent several days. On one of them, it was necessary for me to make dinner. We had a few hens left here by the previous owner. I prepared a big one along with two ground hogs I shot. (In Pennsylvania, groundhogs were considered good food.) I cut them all up into chunks and made a pot roast along with potatoes. Everybody ate like hogs and commented on the good meal. Someone asked what it was. I told them. Half wouldn't believe it, and the other half wanted to fight me.

– B.C. Ahouse

#262 – Friday March 30, 2001

Until recently, I have suffered from relapses of malarial fever. Mostly at home or work. I list a few occasions when this was most noticeable to others. One time, while we were staying at the home of our friends Toney and Misty Izbicki in Glen Lyon, I had a spell that was very noticeable and which he still comments about. Another time while at the Gentlemen's Club in Cherokee, Oklahoma with Fred Cormarck, I suffered a bad time. After having dinner at the Franklin Hotel in Watkins Glen, NY, Irene and I started for our car and I barely made it, being hit hard while crossing the street. Another time while returning from a trip and going through Ithaca at night, I was hit again. I spotted a drug store, parked, went in and asked the druggist if he would sell me some quinine sulphate. He took one look at me and said, "I better do that." He did.

—B.C. Ahouse

#263 – Friday March 30, 2001

Over the years that my four children attended South Seneca schools, I tried to keep aloof of their daily experiences. There was one incident worth recording involving son, Martin, and his fourth grade teacher, Ms. Riley. It seemed she had a fetish for picking on Martin—such as making him stand in the corner in a wastebasket. My wife Irene took it upon herself to resolve the matter. Ms. Riley was not cooperative, simply stating it was a conflict of personalities (in 4th grade?). Irene went to a board director, a druggist in Interlaken, who told her if she didn't keep Martin in school, she would be jailed. After I talked to him, I heard very little of the matter.

—B.C. Ahouse

#264 – Friday March 30, 2001

Beginning in 1948, while working for and learning the pipe felling trade with my brother-in-law Drew Link, I have handled and worked with asbestos in many forms—from plain raw asbestos to manufactured forms. I was never told of its hazards. However, in the 1970s, the problem became known. About 1980, I was working in North Carolina, leasing land for the gas and oil business, where I became acquainted with a cooperative, likable fellow by the name of Dick Baily. His family owned, among many things, an asbestos quarry. He downplayed the threat of asbestos, saying he was always exposed to it with no known problems. But about two years later his wife called to tell me Dick had died of cancer problems caused by the asbestos. A few years ago, Dr. Lorns Merachrueyer of Ithaca said my respiratory problem was most likely caused by asbestos.

—B.C. Ahouse

#265 – Friday March 30, 2002

I recall two times that I was slapped in the face which left a lasting impression. The first was when I was probably about 12 years old. I was up on the second mountain behind the Bliss Colliery and had cut some Mountain Laurel for my mother. We were stopped by two game wardens on Middle Road who were quite abusive. I waved the laurel at one, who promptly slapped me down.

The other time was when in Nanticoke High School, we were having a quiz on Roman history. The answer being "proscriptions." The fellow on the carpet didn't have a clue, so to help, out of turn, I said "prescriptions," whereupon our history teacher "Doc" Richardson promptly slapped me in the face. Moral: Don't act or speak out of turn.

—B.C. Ahouse

#266 – Saturday March 31, 2001

In early 1936, I was offered a job on the Central Railroad of New Jersey on the Nanticoke Branch because of the heavy snow. Also, I mention that the temperature hovered around zero degrees Fahrenheit for six weeks. Because of the chance to earn money (40 cents per hour), I took about two months out of my junior year in Nanticoke High School. When the job was over, I returned to school, since I wanted to graduate. The only objection was from my commercial ed teacher, Vic Jones. Pleading did no good, so I said if I couldn't pass the current test, I'd leave. I passed the test and returned to school. I have two report cards for that year. At my 58th class reunion, Vic Jones was there but didn't recall this incident.

—B.C. Ahouse

#267 – Saturday March 31, 2001

Clarence "Snaps" Aton was a fellow Gandy dancer on the CNJRR in 1941-1942. He did a lot of reminiscing about the railroad and other jobs he had held. One thing that stuck with me was his relating a period of time he spent at Glen Summit, Pennsylvania (an elite area), where his job was a hospice caretaker for a Mr. Kirby, who started Kirby stores. Clarence said his main concern was to keep Mr. Kirby from having sex with a goat, which was Kirby's pet. While I was in the U.S. Army, Snaps took a different job as a track *** . He had a small gas-powered cart. One day, near the workout between Rita and Whitehaven, PA, he was overtaken by a train and was killed while he was trying to remove the car from the track.

— B.C. Ahouse

#268 – Saturday March 30, 2001

Irene and I raised four fine children: Karl, Susan, Nancy, and Martin. I, "we," tried to instill in them old-fashioned convictions, which I believe they absorbed and retain. I recall telling them that they could have anything they wanted if they worked for it (not 'everything'), but in some cases this may have been a misconception. I was instrumental in helping organize a Lutheran Church in Interlaken, and they all four went through the process of being confirmed as Lutherans. Exposure to our school system and their peers probably nullified this effort. In any report, all four in their own selves are intelligent and productive people. One thing I never did was to interfere or intrude in any of their marriages, since I deemed it useless.

—B.C. Ahouse

#269 – Sunday April 1, 2001

This may be a one-of-a-kind incident, so I have set it down. My Uncle Gus Brush, on whose farm I often stayed to work or hunt, is the basis of this "tale." Gus had a flock of ducks, about ten drakes and two hens. The hens were probably abused until they made a nest and each sat on them to incubate their eggs. The drakes were not to be deprived, so in some sort of drive or intellect they cooperated in the following manner. The drakes would take turns chasing a checker hen until she tired, whereupon two drakes would take a wing each and hold her prostrate while some of the others would enjoy their breeding prowess. This is true, I saw it many times.

—B.C. Ahouse

#270 – Sunday April 1, 2001

About 25 years ago, while visiting with Irene's relatives in Lake Worth, Florida, we were out for a drive around the area with Irene's Uncle John and Aunt Mae Vetter. They were expecting John's sister Madeline and her husband Bill K in from Loveland, Colorado some time soon. While we were passing a gas station on the military trail, I spotted a Colorado car and said, "That looks like Bill driving." John pulled over across the road. I went up to the car, recognized Bill and welcomed him to Florida. He didn't recognize me and asked how anybody knew he was Bill K. I explained and how John was parked across the street.

He said, "What luck, now I don't have to look for his house." I got back into John's car and told him Bill would follow him home. For some reason John drove off fast and Bill couldn't keep up and lost John. It took Bill all night to find John's house.

— B.C. Ahouse

#271 – Sunday April 1, 2001

Once, when my cousin Ted Brush was a young teenager, our Uncle Leo *** happened to say that because of all the cats that were around that no matter what you did to a cat, he would always land on his feet when you threw him up into the air. To test this theory, Ted got a large tire and a cat and took them up on the hill behind the house. He put the cat in the tire and rolled it about 500 feet down the hill. He ran after it, got the cat out and threw it up in the air. The poor cat had no facilities and landed on its head. It lay there. Ted called Uncle Leo to see the cat on the ground and said, "Uncle Leo, you are a darn liar."

— B.C. Ahouse

#272 – Sunday April 1, 2001

As I indicated in a previously penned poem, I do not believe there is such a thing as animal rights. By the same token, I don't believe anyone should ever abuse a fellow creature or willingly allow them to abuse each other. Some fools maintain that an animal will only kill what it needs for food. I hereby recite some occurrences that I witnessed and can swear to.

Back in the late 1940s early 1950s, I had several range corps housing pullets in the orchard west of my house. One Sunday morning, as I went to feed them, I saw a red fox in the west end of the lot. Upon investigating, I found he had killed 40 or 50 pullets.

Another time I moved a range coop south of the house into an oat field to clean up wind-downed grain. A flock of hawks killed them all.

Once, in a breeder house, I went in to find dozens of the baby chicks killed. They were being eaten by a dwarf male rat whose testicles were way beyond normal size.

—B.C. Ahouse

#273 – Sunday April 1, 2001

In the kitchen to the left of the outside door in my Uncle Gus's house, there was a couch that everybody seemed to enjoy stretching out on. This was OK until it evolved into a fight as to who was going to enjoy it. This was usually between Gus, his son Ted, Avis (his wife), and his brother John. One day, I was alone with Aunty Avis, she asked me to help her move the couch out into the milk house, which I did. This left the area by the door bare. Later that day, as each of them came into the kitchen, first Ted, then John, then Gus, without looking threw themselves supposedly onto the couch, but instead landed on the hard floor with a thud.

—B.C. Ahouse

#274 – Monday April 2, 2001

As I mentioned before, I spent quite a bit of time with my Uncle Gus Brush and his wife Avis. This was most likely the best home life I ever experienced to this time. My cousin Marion was always a pleasant girl and a joy to know. She was never very shy, but one day when I came home, she was alone in the kitchen and didn't say a word. After a while, I asked if anything was wrong and she just shook her head. I was a little concerned and asked her to say something, whereupon she put her hands up to her mouth an into them emptied a full box of Bluch Smith Brother Cough Drops.

—B.C. Ahouse

#275 – Monday April 2, 2001

I stopped at the Ritchie House one mile east of Interlaken one day to see Mrs. Ritchie about some land business. I stood aside while she had a discussion with a fellow who came in a truck with a mare in it. It seemed that he had bought the horse from Mrs. Ritchie with the guarantee that it was in foal (pregnant). Mrs. Ritchie insisted that it was (a mare doesn't usually show signs like a cow does) and their argument became quite heated. I walked around the truck and what I noticed prompted me to call both parties over to observe the first sign of the mare giving birth to a colt. Apparently, the truck ride from Pennsylvania had encouraged the mare's labor.

— B.C. Ahouse

#276 – Tuesday April 3, 2001

It was the late 1940s, and we had a family of houseguests. Irene's NY City friend Evelyn Doir and her husband Sydney, a British merchant sailor. As luck had it, they got snowed in with us in one of the biggest storms we ever had here. One day, Sydney said, "Why don't I let the dogs in the house to get warm?"

I said, "It's warmer in the cow barn, that's good enough for them."

Anyway, he opened the door to let the small poodle-like dog in, got romping with her, and as luck had it, she threw up on the kitchen floor. Whereupon Pooch, our young Airedale, came in, which he seldom ever did, and ate the mess on the floor. To make matters worse, Sydney then threw up too.

— B.C. Ahouse

#277 – Monday April 2, 2001

In the middle 1970s, we were traveling through western Arkansas, going east from Fort Smith. We encountered the wine area and spent the night at a winery, having dinner there. The next day, as we started out, we saw a sign advertising a ranch for sale by the owners. We stopped in. The lady of the house invited Irene in but cautioned her to watch out for the rattlesnake in the yard. Her husband, she told me, was up in a hill field with some cattle. Mr. Favor, his name, was having some trouble with a Simmental heifer which was having trouble calving. I offered my help—if wanted. We turned the animal, which was on its side, so that her head was up hill. With the aid of gravity, I applied some pressure on her bulging abdomen, and in a short time the calf arrived in good shape. Favor sure thanked me. He was a retired oil man who was reluctant to be a rancher.

—B.C. Ahouse

#278 – Monday April 2, 2001

To follow-up, I asked my newfound friend why he chose Arkansas over Texas to retire. He said because he was 18 years old before he knew you didn't have to live with dirt in your eyes. He was an oil-field man who spent much time in South America and related some tales from there. In Tierra del Fuego, the island off the southern tip, he said the giant Nutwa, who were naked when discovered, were clothed by the do-good missionaries. Whereby, in swimming the channel, they got soaked and most died from the freeze of the clothes. In Venezuela, he told of helping a rancher load cattle for market with his side boom. It seems they threw and tied the animals and took them to market on the flatbed truck on their sides. As a reward, the rancher took Favor on a trip up the Orinoco River as he transported some diamond buyers. One native had a large green stone; the buyer said, "My god, it's a green one," whereby the native took it out of his hand and threw it in the river.

— B.C. Ahouse

#279 – Monday April 2, 2001

Have you ever wondered why dogs chase cats? Well, I know exactly why one did. As Uncle Gus was putting his cows across the road to pasture, a half-grown kitten followed him. As the cows crossed the road, a Great Dane dog ran up to the herd, noticed the cat, chased it down, grabbed it in his mouth, chomped on it and swallowed the kitten whole. Gus saw all of this, picked up a fencepost, and struck the dog across its back, never phasing it in its stride. Another time, I was walking to my grandmother's house from Gus's with Grandma's dog, Kernel. We passed a house whose owners had a cat, Dorie, which came running out towards us. Kernel, who I never knew to shirk a fight, took one look, put his tail between his legs and ran.

— B.C. Ahouse

#280 – Monday April 2, 2001

About 30 years ago, while in Florida, we (my family and I) visited a former Lutheran minister, Don Schroeder, who was the pastor of the Lutheran church in Stuart. He gave us a tour of the church with its rose garden, and then mentioned that he had recently married Jim Rand Sr. I said I knew him — Rand — casually, and Don offered to take us out to his place, which had been a mobile oil property. On the way out, we stopped at an old lighthouse post that was then a turtle conservatory. Interestingly enough, the fellow who was in charge, a Bill Alloway, was an old friend of mine from my days at Remington Rand in Johnson City, NY. We renewed our acquaintance and he gave us a tour of the turtle conservatory. Jim Rand was not home. However, this property of his was developed into exclusive homes. One was accepted by Bill Rousoldt.

— B.C. Ahouse

#281 – Monday April 2, 2001

Lenin is well-known for his expression that religion is the opiate of the masses. Whatever his reasoning, it did not help in the long-term survival of his soviet communism. However, it is now appropriate I believe, to say that sports have replaced it as the opiate of the masses. Too much emphasis and money is heaped on the various games. I believe, however, that basketball, while entertaining to some, is the most ridiculous sport. The Watusi games of our black friends gave them control of the sport. Why not use the politically correct affirmative action idea to include more of other colors? Another thought would be to raise the basket to adjust for the abnormal height of the average player. Maybe religion was the best opiate after all.

—B.C. Ahouse

#282 – Monday April 2, 2001

During the winter of 1940-1941, I and my Uncle William Suntken, worked in Baltimore at Ft. Holabird as carpenters. We were later joined by my brother-in-law Drew Link, who was a plumber. We rented a room from a Ms. Jean Free on Eutaw Street, right off of North Ave. It was a large room in a well-built old house. After a while, it became apparent that some of the rooms served as a brothel, which was something strange to me. Anyhow, there were two men, always well dressed, who passed themselves off as salesmen. One evening, they came in in high spirits and invited us to a party to help celebrate their good luck at one of the local racetracks. That party was my first taste of champagne. It was broken up, however, when the house was raided by a large police force. It seems these men had, that afternoon, robbed a bank.

—B.C. Ahouse

#283 – Tuesday April 3, 2001

The other day on TV news, there was some mention of a dog fight that was raided, and the fact that one of the dead dogs had one of his feet cut off, which puzzled the commentator. This prompted me to recall a tale that my old Army friend, Gersham "Sarge" Phillips, from Benton, Arkansas once told me. He was a fellow who traded in dogs along with timber and other things. Once, one of his friends told me that Sarge made his sizeable fortune trading in coon dogs (it was timber). He must have attended and maybe traded in dogs for the fighting pits. This one time, a bitch was pitted against another, who was chewing her up. The bitch locked on to the stronger dog's leg, and to demonstrate her tenacity, the owner cut off her foot, where upon she did not relinquish her grip on her attacker. This made her pups more valuable.

— B.C. Ahouse

#284 – Tuesday April 3, 2001

My friend Jim Teemly ran a butcher's shop in Watkins Glen which had been previously owned by his father. Jim took a lot of kidding, like the time his dad was caught lacing the oysters with spring water when a small frog showed up in the container. Anyway, one day, when I entered the shop, Jim seemed to be in better spirits than his usual good self. I asked him what was new. He said his boy just showed him his latest report card. I asked how the young fellow was doing. Jim said, "He's now the smartest kid in the dumb class." Jim and family are of the best.

—B.C. Ahouse

#285 – Tuesday April 3, 2001

About 25 years ago, a group of Buddha type people from Watkins Glen approached me through a mutual friend. They were preparing to build a temple in Hector, which they did. I sold them enough hemlock trees to do so, for which they paid me $1,000. I cautioned them about their design, wherein the walls were too long. I suggested two square buildings, which they built, connecting the two. They also came back for another tree, which had quite a bend to it, and offered me $100, which I accepted. As erected thus, it meant friendship or something such.

My friend tried to get me involved in their practices, which included sorts of yoga. I watched some of it. After being positioned sitting cross-legged, my friend got up, or tried to, and broke his leg trying.

— B.C. Ahouse

#286 – Wednesday April 4, 2001

I met Walter Hill, of Greenbay or Reinlander, Wisconsin, through my second father-in-law, John Olsen. This occurred in Florida, where we visited and enjoyed some floor shows in proper restaurants. Walter's wife commented about the showgirls and how it was so deplorable that they couldn't have received an education and a better position in life. Walter replied, "And maybe become a schoolteacher like you." Walter ran an oil business in Wisconsin and I recall his describing it as lopsided in profits. He said he made his money trucking fuel from St. Paul-Minneapolis, Minnesota to Reinlander, which made up for the poor returns that he received on the local deliveries to the retail customers. All in all, it was a pleasure to make his acquaintance.

— B.C. Ahouse

#287 – Thursday April 5, 2001

A little over a year ago, my brother, Alfred Ahouse, was traveling west with his companion, June Kenyan, on their way to a Green Bay Packers football game. While having dinner in South Bend, Indiana, Alfred had a cardiac attack and for all practical purposes was dead. By good luck, there was a physician and a medic in the restaurant who were able to restore Al's heartbeat. Al was taken to a hospital, where with remarkable care, he survived, and is today able to function very well. He had a defibrillator installed in his body. Although I talked to Al while he was in the hospital in Indiana, he tells me that he does not recall anything after leaving NY or returning here.

— B.C. Ahouse

#288 – Thursday April 5, 2001

When our son Martin was two or three years old, we were vacationing in Florida, staying with my in-laws, John and Tillie Olson, in Lakeworth. One Sunday afternoon, we drove down to Ft. Lauderdale to visit a Lodi, NY neighbor who had inherited a house there. He took us for a tour of his house and garden. While Stan Wagner and I were talking about the tall coconut trees, Martin, who was wandering about, came running up to me. As he came to a halt, a full-sized coconut dropped from a tree about 30 feet high and came within inches of striking the top of Martin's head.

—B.C. Ahouse

#289 – Friday April 6, 2001

About 20 years ago or so, there was a glut of concord grapes and this resulted in there being a lot of unharvested grapes remaining on the vines in the vineyards of the Finger Lakes, NY. My friend, Dave Barber, was one of these fellows who had done so with the result of the grapes fermenting on the vine. Wild turkeys were then returning to our area, and they included grapes in their diet. This resulted in a hen becoming intoxicated and falling into a stupor. Dave caught her and thought of pulling a joke on a mutual friend, Don Tillinghast, who was an avid turkey hunter. Dave put the turkey in the back of his car and drove to Lodi, where Don worked for Porters. During the short trip from Valois, the hen sobered up, came awake and wild and made a filthy mess crapping in Dave's car.

— B.C. Ahouse

#290 – Friday April 6, 2001

In the early 1960s, we were returning from a vacation with Irene's mother Tillie in the 1960 Rambler Irene had inherited from her father Adolf. While traveling north through Daytona Beach, FL, we noticed smoke in the car. I pulled over to the curb, opened the trunk, and saw that the wire under the rear seat had shorted out and was burning the upholstery. I managed to put the fire out, insulate the wires, and go on our way. I considered their poor workmanship in manufacture, as it was a fairly new car. Also to mention, the front wheel kingpins had no proper bearings—only a bolt resting on a nut. Irene lost one front wheel in front of the Peterson house that summer—more bad work. I repaired the assembly myself with a replacement kit.

—B.C. Ahouse

#291 – Saturday April 7, 2001

I have witnessed several tragedies in the past. The first being when I was a young boy of eight or nine. We were at a family reunion of sorts at San Souer Park in Hanover Township, PA. A lady in a neighboring group laid her young baby on a small blanket on the ground. She had just turned away when a large towing car came in and crushed the child. Another time, in the mid-1930s, I was having supper at my Aunt Emma and Uncle Fred MacLaughlin's kitchen in Nuangola, PA. Their landlord, Foster Stouer, came in to pick up the rent. As usual, he was in a hurry, got into his car outside my right window and backed over the young boy from next door, mangling him up in his tricycle. Another time, about 1950, I went to the drugstore in Shavertown, PA. A school bus had just stopped and let some kids out. One little boy lost his cap, which blew under the bus, where he tried to get it, and the bus ran over him. Three tragic deaths.

— B.C. Ahouse

#292 – Monday April 9, 2001

During the summer of 1941, while at a square dance at Fey's Grove in Dorrance, PA, we went outside during the intermission. The sky to the north was starting to show signs of the Northern Lights (the Aurora Borealis). At first, it was a light pink, then it darkened to a deep red and spread out to the east and west. I have never seen anything like it, nor did anybody else who was there. Someone remarked that he hoped it wasn't a sign of a bloodbath in the war, which seemed eminent. Two fellows there that night, Victor Sanchuries and Cul Eisenhower, I believe both were lost in World War II.

—B.C. Ahouse

#293 – Monday April 9, 2001

About 1974, I had employed a former neighbor (and I thought friend), George Ray Cannon, to install the electric systems in several houses I built after the 1972 flood in the Elmira-Corning area. As mentioned before, and I will again, I had some bad relations with the banks I was dealing with in the area. Ray sensed this and came to me to be paid off and quit. I said, "OK, I owe you $1,500 and I'll give you a check." He said no way, I owed him $5,000. I said I didn't. He retained attorney Henry Valent of Watkins Glen, who took me to court there. After several days of Henry and my attorney, Bill Ruger bothering the court, I turned to Judge Jankovitch and asked if I could tell the honest truth and wrap this up. He said OK. I gave my side of the story. The jury deliberated, came out in favor of Ray Cannon and said I owed him $50, which I promptly paid. Henry looked sick. Ray had a stroke, which I was blamed for.

—B.C. Ahouse

#294 – Monday April 9, 2001

My son Karl and Darlene Close were married in the late 1970s and had their wedding reception in the Masonic Hall in Lodi. With over a hundred people in attendance, Deputy Sheriff Jim Bond came in shouting at the top of his voice for me, Bernard Ahouse, "I have three subpoenas for him." This was an embarrassment, which I related to the sheriff. He sent Bond to apologize, which I didn't accept. The subpoenas were from the Columbia S&L bank, who had installed a computer system which put me in default. I protested and ended up in court in Rochester. I maintained that I was not in default. The judge listened to the bank's lawyers, said that he would sooner believe Bernard Ahouse, and dismissed their three actions for foreclosure. My attorney said he had never seen such a thing before. I later handled this in my favor.

—B.C. Ahouse

#295 – Tuesday April 10, 2001

Once again, may I reflect on the integrity of an attorney. Bill Ruger handled the aforementioned Ray Canon case. Perhaps he was annoyed by my speaking to Judge Jankovitch. Anyway, I had a problem with Marine Midland Bank, who was trying to cheat me out of $25,000 with the collusion of Elmira Savings Bank and a Mr. and Mrs. Geedon Hubeit, who had purchased a house from me. Bill approached me one day wanting to tell me that besides being a fine attorney, he was also an excellent businessman, which was why he was dropping my case and was going to heretofore represent Marine Midland Bank. He simply said they had made him a better offer.

— B.C. Ahouse

#296 – Tuesday April 10, 2001

Irene and I bought a 1996 Ford Crown Victoria, a program car from Lucchesi Ford of Waterloo, NY. This car was driven by Irene, and I bought it for her satisfaction. There was a slight rumble in it, which was immediately pointed out to Steve and Dave Lucchesi to no avail. I was told it was the tires, which they said were not their responsibility. Over the years, I changed all of the tires, which only made the vibration worse. The tires were chewed up. The vibration also cracked the windshield twice. The last trip I made to NJ resulted in a lump developing on my right hand. Changing the transmission fluid and filter finally partly corrected the problem. I turned this all over to Ford CEO Jacques Nasser.

—B.C. Ahouse

#297 – Friday April 13, 2001

With full emphasis towards those many who cannot or will not accept God as the maker of heaven and earth, I present the reason for my convictions. Of all the common elements and compounds that I know of, there is only one that expands on freezing and on heating, and that is water—H_2O. It is easy to see that if water, like other materials, shrank on cooling or freezing, it would sink to the bottom of any body of water and most likely stay there. The world would then end up a frozen mass with little chance of life of any sort or movement of any tides.

—B.C. Ahouse

#298 – Monday April 16, 2001

There was a comic strip by Johnny Hail in the news several days before it came out in the paper. The Jewish community didn't think it funny. Whether it is or not, I believe it was created by the author as a protest against what seems to be an organized collusion by so-called intellectual Hebrew scholars to belittle the life and existence, much less the teaching, of Jesus—an organized effort by the Jews to further their own agenda. Whatever that may be, question? Is Jewry a religion, a political effort, or a commercial enterprise? Religion seems to be the common denominator. If it is, why does the USA support Israel financially?

—B.C. Ahouse

#299 – Wednesday April 18, 2001

I have visited Independence Hall many times. I believe the first was in 1938 when I stopped in Philly to visit my cousin Jules Kuhn on my way home from Cape May, NJ.

I was much impressed by the good condition the place was in.

About 1980 when leasing gas and oil properties in North Carolina and Tennessee, I learned that some virgin white pine in that area had been cut to refurbish the Independence Hall. It matched the original pine.

About 40 years ago or so, I took my family to sightsee in Philly which included the Hall. The most memorable event on that occasion was my daughter Susan's curiosity of the Liberty Bell and getting her finger stuck in the crack. A guard produced some lotion and helped her escape, warning not to do that again.

—B.C. Ahouse

#300 – Saturday April 21, 2001

I mention this incident simply because I don't believe many if any ever experienced a similar circumstance. In the dim past, Karl, my son, and I delivered hay to a horse farmer in Owego. This was managed by George Montgomery, who some said was the movie star once married to Dinah Shore. On one occasion, while George was showing me around the barns we came up to a veterinarian who was working on the tail end of a horse. This person was dressed in coveralls with the hood up because of the cold. I approached and said, "What are you doing to that mare, fella?" This attractive lady turned to me and said, "Why I'm suturing her vagina."

—B.C. Ahouse

#301 – Monday April 23, 2001

Twenty-some years ago, Irene and I were staying at a motel in Key West, Florida. We went out to dinner at the extreme end of the road along the water to a restaurant that served good seafood. After dinner, there came in a three-piece band who put on a good show. During an interlude, one of the boys asked if anyone present was from upstate New York. I, as usual, spoke up and said, "Sure." They asked where from and I said, "Lodi," whereupon the three fellows came down to our table. They were friends with our son Martin. Their father had been the principal of Romulus Central School. They were the MacDonalds. Chris later became a movie star in *Thelma and Louise*. Pete became *** in *** and *** video business as did the other brother in *** .

—B.C. Ahouse

#302 – Monday April 23, 2001

On our way out to Key West one year, we stopped at a Holiday Inn in *** FL, south of Miami. It was a good inn but the only place where they tried to charge me for long distance calls that I didn't make. They said they would call the police. I said, "OK, I have someone to call too." That was the end of that. Down the road a little there was a fair of some sort going on which we took in. They were displaying an American flag that was claimed to be the biggest ever made. It was quite high but unbelievably someone stole it that night. Hard to believer but true.

—B.C. Ahouse

#303 – Thursday April 26, 2001

Irene's cousin Marilyn was married to Dick Conlon, who lived in north Chicago. They had two girls and a boy, who has recovered from cancer. When the children were young, they were allowed to have some hamsters and gerbils as pets. As nature has its way, they were soon overrun with the pets' offspring. Marilyn called several pet shops to see if they might want them. None did, but they suggested taking them to the Chicago Zoo. This they did and the keepers gladly accepted them. After unloading the lot and as they were about to leave, one of the zoo men said, "Wouldn't you all like to watch us feed the wolves with your gift?"

— B.C. Ahouse

#304 – Friday April 27, 2001

My associate Bill Rousoldt had an option to buy the El Capitan Ranch in Santa Barbara, CA. When at the Pegasus Ranch in Florida, he asked me to examine the deed. It seemed incomplete in regard to various rights, so he assigned me to sort it out. Both Texaco and Exxon had interest in the area because of the enormous oil deposits off shore; this was heavy oil and high in sulfur. Exxon had plans for an enormous refinery to the north and needed rights through the El Capitan Ranch for pipelines. I endeavored to put the two together. I also contacted the local U.S. congressmen, but to no avail. The *** mounted a *** against the plant and also against the pipeline to carry gas to Los Angeles. I also *** the Trust for Public land in San Francisco through Margaret *** . To my knowledge, nothing materialized. *** could probably use the gas.

—B.C. Ahouse

#305 – Friday April 27, 2001

One of the oddest things that ever happened to me occurred in a restaurant where we came in for breakfast after a night in the nearby motel. We were seated at a table and after we enjoyed a cup of coffee, the waitress came along with two glasses of water. She set one on the table for Irene and as she walked around to my side, she stubbed her foot, upsetting the tray with the other glass of water on it. I reached out and grabbed the glass, which was now upside down. It landed in the palm of my hand and I don't believe a drop was spilled. The waitress said that must be a miracle. True.

— B.C. Ahouse

Bernard C. Ahouse

#306 thru #312 not included in handwritten sheets.
To be added later.

320

#313 – Friday June 1, 2001

I have just read a magazine account by Rosie O'Donnell about a staph infection she picked up in a hospital. This involved a finger on her left hand. It prompted me to recall what Dr. Steguso called blood poisoning that infected my left hand. I had pinched it between a nail set and a hammer as I was setting nails on a porch banister we were building in Rita, New York. The doctor lanced it between my thumb and forefinger whereby he extracted a good cup of puss from it. It left my hand weakened and my left forefinger prone to withdraw away from the rest of my fingers sort of creating a V-shape with both my middle and forefinger. It has always made it necessary to use extra care when picking something up.

— B.C. Ahouse

#314 – Monday June 4, 2001

I just previously mentioned the damage done to my left hand and how the forefinger pulls to the thumb as I open it up. I mentioned this to my daughter Nancy yesterday and asked if she had ever noticed the condition of my left hand. She said that she had never done so. This incident happened 60 years ago, and to my knowledge only one person has noticed what I mentioned. This was a lady who worked in the defense plant in Johnson City where I spent the last year of World War II. She commented and discussed it with me. One time, I was sent to a doctor who was to evaluate me for an injury I received on a power plant in Binghamton. He told me to stretch my arms out and to bring my forefingers together. As they didn't touch with my eyes closed, he said I was faking and left me alone.

—B.C. Ahouse

#315 – Monday June 4, 2001

About 1960, when I was assisting in organizing the Lutheran Church in Interlaken, NY, I was chaperoning Don Schroeder, our pastor, about the countryside. We stopped at the Rondemakis' home (now owned and occupied by attorney Lawrence Reverby). Mrs. Rondemaki invited us in but was quite cool to us, as was the nature of some Finnish people. When Pastor Schroeder mentioned the cross that Jesus bore for us, she lost it and took us into her daughter's bedroom to show the cross she had borne for 30 years. The poor person was comatose in the bed and as thin as a rail. The most pitiful person I have ever seen. Mrs. Rondemaki had nursed her for years without any outside help as far as I could see. Schroeder was speechless.

— B.C. Ahouse

#316 – Tuesday June 12, 2001

Sorry, I cannot make any of this one out.

#317 – Saturday June 16, 2001

Sorry, I can make out little if any of this one out.

#318 – Monday June 25, 2001

My sister Almena, who died in childbirth while I was in the Army, was married to Drew Link, a plumber who I worked for at times. Drew had a brother, Arthur, who I ran into while working in Baltimore. Art was a glad-hand man for Bath Iron Works in Bath, Maine. One of his chores was *** property, for which he had an expense account. On occasion, Art would treat me to dinner. One matter that sticks in my mind was Art's method of dealing with a bad meal or bad manners by the waiter. He carried a cockroach in a matchbox, and to maximize the complaint he would slip the insect under the remains of his meal and simply say that he couldn't conscientiously pay for such service.

— B.C. Ahouse

#319 – Monday June 25, 2001

Over the years, I have heard much discussion about the affection of pets to their owners, re: cats and dogs. I want to record the recollections of my cousin Luther Domain, a police officer in Houston, Texas for many years. Luther has told me that on many occasions when a person had died along with a dog, the dog would invariably be alongside the deceased as if in mourning. However, he told me that if a cat did not have sufficient food available, they would most always gnaw away at the deceased corpse.

—B.C. Ahouse

#320 – Wednesday June 27, 2001

Fred Cormack was an acquaintance once in the National Conservationists Movement in the U.S. He was a rancher in Oklahoma, a friend of Bud Tucker, who often entertained us there and other places. Fred was a member of the Oklahoma Prison Board and also, I believe, the Banking Commission.

About 20 years ago or so, there was a serious riot in (I believe) the Eastern Oklahoma Penitentiary, whereby all the windows were destroyed. About Christmas, I talked to Fred and asked if the windows were repaired before the winter set in. He said no, they would be replaced in the spring when the weather was better.

—B.C. Ahouse

#321 – Wednesday June 27, 2001

I was born and raised in the city of Nanticoke in Luzerne County, Pennsylvania. We never had any black residents there until a family moved into a house on Railroad Street, facing the Susquehanna River. They became so self-indignant when almost everybody in town came down to check them out that they moved away.

Anyway, when I first traveled south in the late 1930s, I happened to come upon two black fellows who were having a vicious fistfight. For the life of me, I could not figure out how they could possibly have anything to fight about—they seemed so alike to me.

—B.C. Ahouse

#322 – Tuesday July 3, 2001

Lately there has been mention of professional dog fighting on the TV. One occasion involved a dog with an amputated foot. This prompted me to recall a matter related to me by Gersham "Sarge" Phillips of Benton, Arkansas, who was an old friend from WW II days.

Sarge was a wealthy land speculator who was also a coon hunter and a dealer of dogs. One friend of his told me he made his money dealing dogs. Anyway, Sarge told me that in selling a dog for breeding purposes (female) the practice was to cut a foot off with a knife to show how she wouldn't release a death grip on another dog even because of the pain she was in.

— B.C. Ahouse

#323 – Saturday July 7, 2001

Our friend Mrs. Charlotte Seely, who was Irene's brother-in-law Tom Seely's mother, was a fine lady and mother of five boys and two girls. Mrs. Seely was a schoolteacher and well thought of in Trumansburg, where she taught school. One summer's day while visiting us during hay season, as we were sitting on the porch, a young employee of ours, Sammy Bradley, happened to pass by on his way to the barns. Mrs. Seely piped right up exclaiming, "Why that's Sammy Bradley. What is he doing here?"

I said, "Working, what's the problem?"

She said, "Why he is in my retard class in school?"

I said, "I can't believe it. What is his handicap?"

She said, "Why he's only interested in girls older than he is."

—B.C. Ahouse

#324 – Saturday July 7, 2001

Since my service in World War II, I have been plagued with bouts of dysentery — sometimes severe. I was examined by many doctors who usually suggested eliminating something from my diet. Irene's stepfather-in-law, John Olson, suggested gin, which helped on occasion. After the bad spell my wife endured in the Geneva Hospital in 1994, I developed an ulcer. After Dr. Munchweyer examined me, he prescribed an expensive series of antibiotics for the bacteria. These cured the ulcer and to the disbelief of Dr. Munchweyer, it also cured my dysentery. A new experience which I just recently managed to control. I might add that the food I was told to eliminate left me nothing to eat.

— B.C. Ahouse

#325 – Thursday July 12, 2001

There have been three helicopter crashes hereabouts in the last several years, two of them fatal. This brings to mind one occasion probably 20 years ago. While I was going east on the Searsburg Road after leaving the Lane Farms, which we owned, the fog thickened as I went up the hill. Just west of the Warren County Road, I heard a low-flying helicopter which prompted me to stop so I wouldn't run into it if it happened to land on the road. As luck had it, it landed on the northeast corner of the two mentioned roads. Two men got out and were relieved to be safe. They said they would wait till the fog lifted.

—B.C. Ahouse

#326 – Saturday July 14, 2001

Pro-abortionists are called pro-choice in the media. It should be pro-death. I am against abortion as a matter of convenience for irresponsible people. There are undoubtedly legal reasons for a abortion. I propose a method of controlling this. Since births, marriages, divorces, and deaths are routinely reported in the newspapers, why not report abortions also? This would be no more a possible embarrassment to a woman than the published report of a birth to an unwed woman. Apparently, political correctness and social engineering play a role here, which are viewed as an invasion of privacy.

— B.C. Ahouse

#327 – Monday July 16, 2001

About 20 years ago, we in Seneca County began to welcome an influx of Amish families, who were enticed by the relatively inexpensive good farmland. At that time, I was working as a land man for the gas and oil business with my associate Charles A. "Chuck" Lucido. The Amish people as a whole welcomed the possibility of income from a gas well. One fellow, Henry Esh, gladly accepted the lease I offered. I had occasion to visit him on several occasions. I mention this because of the Esh's twin girls, barely one year old and identical except for the fact that one gladly came to me to be picked up and the other ran to a corner in the room and began to cry. Identicalness stopped there.

— B.C. Ahouse

#328 – Thursday July 26, 2001

Recently there has been some news about patent rights involving the modern helicopter. When I was a young boy in Nanticoke, PA, we had a neighbor, a Mike Bigda, who was the owner of an autogyro, which he kept at the Wyoming Valley Airport. This was a single wing (low) plane with two cockpit seats. There was a propeller in the front as I remember and a large horizontal propeller blade which towered over the fuselage. The plane could take off and land vertically. I often thought that this was the original helicopter. As I remember, Mike crashed the plane.

—B.C. Ahouse

#329 – Thursday July 26, 2001

With my young children and others, I often theorized about gravity. Karl, my eldest, recently brought this to mind. It was quite obvious to all that although it was a definite attraction, it was not magnetism as we know it. However, without having opposite attraction poles, negative and positive, there must be some identical part of every atom that is attracted to each other. It could be in the center of the atom or perhaps a ring around each or a part of the ring that causes all matter to fall towards the greater mass.

— B.C. Ahouse

#330 – Thursday July 26, 2001

When we bought this farmhouse and farm in 1946, it was lived in by Carl Stewart and his family (two girls and a boy) as I recall. Carl was a genuine fellow who on occasion sported a moustache which he periodically shaved. I wondered about this and finally noticed that when another fellow, Cort Mulford, grew one, Carl shaved his off. One occasion that is worth mentioning regards his wife wanting and buying a piano at a sale in Interlaken. She persuaded a reluctant Carl to bring it home to her. He loaded it on a pickup truck without securing it properly. On turning west in Interlaken to go to Lodi, he used excessive speed and lost the piano, which broke into hundreds of pieces on the road. It sounded like music there for a while afterwards.

—B.C. Ahouse

#331 – Monday July 30, 2001

Over the years, we have installed many miles of tile drainage ditches. One of the trencher contractors was a Mr. Cudlebach. He had a black man by the name of Sam who operated the machine. Sam was a very quiet person but after a while we began to converse. I asked him if he was married. A couple of days later he told me that he used to be. I asked him if we was divorced. He said, "No, we were so mad we didn't need a divorce." It seemed that some year prior to his coming to New York, he farmed in Georgia and the trouble began when he was cultivating a long field of cotton and his wife timed his taking a long drink of water on the far end of the field from her cousin. It apparently took him a minute longer than it did with her.

—B.C. Ahouse

#332 – Friday August 10, 2001

My friend Charles Hendrix was married to my wife Irene's cousin Rose Asay. They both served in the Army in WW II, Charles going through the New Guinea campaign. He told of being in swamps for weeks and finally moving up into the highlands, where they came upon a fast-flowing stream where they filled up with fresh water, boiling it thoroughly. The bad part was when they moved up behind a logjam where were several bloated dead Japs. Charley got home safely and eventually bought a motorcycle. After his attempt to settle up the matters, he said to me, "Well I blew my dollars, now I have to get some sense."

— B.C. Ahouse

#333 – Friday August 10, 2001

Some people have a deadly fear of snakes, two of whom are my wife Irene and son Martin. Once in Galveston, TX at a marina show, a fellow working with a cobra bent over and kissed its head while facing it. Irene almost fainted. On one occasion, while a teenager, and with my brother Al, we were going to see relatives in Shavertown, PA by crossing Kelly Field, where the black creek ran through and turned under the central railroad of NJ. We climbed up the high railroad bank at the crest of the tunnel where dozens of large snakes were gathered in a commingled pile. We had to keep going, as some of them began going down through our legs. Al recalled this a few weeks ago when I mentioned it. Also, the time he shot a rattlesnake on Hatch Mountain, PA and told the fellows in the Lodi saloon that he killed it on the LURR in Lodi. When he changed his story, our friend Russ Snull wouldn't believe it.

—B.C. Ahouse

#334 – Monday August 13, 2001

I had already mentioned some possibly fatal shots while hunting on the part of others. I here wish to mention some lucky shots, or perhaps in reference to the target, unlucky ones. Probably 65 years ago, I was hunting with my three Burman uncles in Mountain Top, PA when Richard decided to shoot his .22 rifle at a hawk which was a good quarter-mile in the sky. His one shot hit it, and it dropped like a rock. Here on my farm in Lodi, a friend, Dave Eastman, and I were returning from a hunt nearby when a lone goose appeared ahead a good 500-600 feet above us. Dave took a random shot and one pellet hit the goose in the head. It came tumbling down. I rather think that the fall killed it.

—B.C. Ahouse

#335 – Thursday August 23, 2001

Having run a dairy when we first began farming in NY, I am well acquainted with the trials and tribulations of that deal. While serving on the State Conservation District Board in Albany in the late 1970s, I made a proposal that it would not be out of line if dairy farmers were pensioned by the state or a relative committee after they had diligently run a dairy for 20 years. The board secretary presented the motion but it was not considered because dairy farmers were not state employees who, as such, were entitled to such lucrative pension. My immediate reply was that dairy farmers contributed much more to the state than the CSEO members.

— B.C. Ahouse

#336 – Thursday August 23, 2001

A newsworthy item that attracted my attention was the matter concerning Governor Casey of PA. As I recall, the governor was in dire need of a heart and lung transplant, but there didn't seem to be any replacement organs available. Probably just as a coincidence, a black man was shot dead by the police in Pittsburgh, according to my recall of the news item relating to this incident. The dead man provided the necessary donation to the governor, who promptly accepted the organs and survived the operation. Thought this was newsworthy.

— B.C. Ahouse

#337 – Monday September 10, 2001

About five years ago or so, when I was in contact with David Hardo, Merv Griffin's CEO in Atlantic City, I was interested in seeing Ray Zayae, the master of ceremonies on the TV *Wheel of Fortune* when he tried to mastermind a late night show in competition with Johnny Carson. It didn't fly or last long. I commented to David that I believe the reason for its failure was that many old folks tuned in to Carson and fell asleep with their TV on, which still counted in the Neilson scale. This gave Carson an unfair count in the Neilson scale.

—B.C. Ahouse

#338 – Monday September 10, 2001

While in Honolulu in 1976, attending the conservation convention, I swam out at Waikiki Beach about a thousand feet to where a couple were standing. I stopped and asked if this was a sandbar. They said no, and explained that it was only four or five feet deep all the way out here. I could have walked. Also, there was a group of sugar growers seeking support for their program of subsidies and quotas of *** . They asked for my support, which I agreed to do. I was severely criticized for doing so, being told that our conservation agenda didn't allow commercial discussion. I said our conservation agenda was an excellent way to support sugar growers economically.

— B.C. Ahouse

#339 – Monday September 17, 2001

I wish to refer back to #202, written on January 16, 2001. With no offense intended to any individual Jew or Arab, I wish to reflect on the political correctness of the U.S. government. Although prayer is not allowed in schools, the separation of state and church does not apply to the Jewish state of Israel because of the control of Congress by the Jewish lobby. The often blind U.S. support of Israel has infuriated some Arab personalities who I see to be directing their anger to the U.S. This whole mess, as we have it today, could have been averted if common sense was applied to the Israel problem.

— B.C. Ahouse

#340 – Wednesday September 19, 2001

I referred to the car insurance problem with Marine Midland Bank regarding my father-in-law Adolf Lentz's Rambler and how I beat the bank. Also, when I sold a house in Horseheads to a Gordon Herbert, who financed it through the Elmira Savings Bank. The Marine Midland Bank did not apply the $25,000 to my mortgage. The bank gave it to Gordon Herbert. I sued the Elmira Savings Bank and won the case after appeal. Interestingly enough, the mortgage discharge finally showed up behind a drawer in the Elmira Courthouse. When Marine Midland attempted to merge with the Hong Kong Shanghai Bank, the present head of the New York Banking Authority, Ms. Muriel Seibut, who I just had just yesterday prevailed with my support and affidavit, was against it. Marine Midland switched from a NY bank to a National affiliate and finally accomplished the merger.

— B.C. Ahouse

#341 – Wednesday September 19, 2001

During the Winter of 1945-1946 I worked as a union carpenter (0.85 per hour) on the Binghamton Building on Clinton Street in Binghamton. Frank O'Connell was the general contractor. The superintendent was a John Morison. I was directed to build the forms for the south wall foundation, part of which was for a liquid glass storage tank. John told me the building width was 120 feet. I generally checked the blueprints and noticed that the surface bend was 26 feet, which made the width 126 feet. I said to John that we should check the width. He told me to do as I was told, so I did. After the concrete yardage was all poured, he realized the mistake and criticized me for not insisting on having him check my figures. Needless to say, the entire south wall was torn out and replaced.

— B.C. Ahouse

#342 – Wednesday September 19, 2001

I before mentioned President Jimmy Carter when I just heard of him through John "Dick" Shield and of his being on David Rockefeller's two foreign relations committees. On one occasion, at an informal gathering, I referred to this without any comment, but it was about the time Carter made an embargo on wheat to Russia because of the Afghanistan invasion. This embargo, as my son Karl recollected the other day after the attack, cost us a lot of money. A lady chimed in and said she didn't have much time for the "swabby" and in her own way described how he was a procurer for Admiral Hiram Rickover, who also must have lusted for women as Carter had adulted.

— B.C. Ahouse

#343 – Thursday September 20, 2001

I have always professed to be a conservationist, not an environmentalist, who I fear are too contaminated by political correctness. I also have contended that I am one of the oldest conservationists in the USA. The proof I have is our family album. I have a photo taken the day I was made a forest guide of Pennsylvania, signed by M. Senayckowicz and Nathan Morgan on April 11, 1933. On that date, I gave the forest guide pledge and signed it "Bernard C Ahouse" while a member of Boy Scout troop 411, which was in St. John's Slovac Lutheran church on Shawnan Street in Nanticoke, PA. I also still have in the album my bronze forest guide badge.

—B.C. Ahouse

#344 – Thursday September 20, 2001

Copyright 1937 by the times header Beverly Hills, CA June 10. The boxer *** strong bear is the champion *** and Max the champion boxer. This fellow Max Schmeling, however, deserves a lot of credit. He has from the start here conducted himself, both in and out of the ring, in a mighty commendable way that has brought nothing but credit on the country. Roosevelt is trying to get rid of Congress. By tonight, he has tried everything he knows. He has hinted, handed them their hat, and almost insults them. The more unwelcome guest has never been none other than Congress's "One Eyed" Connelly — a sweetheart by comparison.

Yours,

Will Rogers

1933 Me Naught Syndicate Inc

— B.C. Ahouse

#345 – Saturday September 22, 2001

It has been noted before about how our government's errors have probably brought about the situation that we find ourselves in today re: the Jewish lobby's control of Congress, as noted in article #339 on September 17, 2001.

The Wall Street Journal published an editorial by Norman Podhoretz attempting to place the blame primarily on the U.S., with Israel apparently being our scapegoat. ***

— B.C. Ahouse

#346 – Tuesday October 9, 2001

With all the psychological rhubarbing about dreams following the Sept. 11-01 tragedy, I am prompted to note two of mine that I consider extraordinary.

Just before I regained consciousness following the so-called kidney operation with Schuyler Memorial Hospital, I vividly recall in a dream three devils (refer to three doctors) prodding my incision with spears.

Another clear recollection is shortly after my mother's (Edith) death I saw her stoop over a grave in Alden, PA where there was a body of a baby who was shrunken like a mummy. Incredibly, both Mom and the baby started to smile, looked at me, nodded and walked away.

— B.C. Ahouse

#347 – Tuesday October 9, 2001

This is a dumb thing to write about, but since I take a bath every day, I think of it every day. Every time I wash my ears, I recall the first time I met a new neighbor on Smith Road in 1946, a Mr. Harry Hatch. Harry was a sophisticated kind of a fellow who came to Lodi from Freehold, New Jersey to run a dairy on the farm that he bought from Joe Swartout. You couldn't help but notice that the inside of Harry's ears were as black as coal. It is a sight that amazed me and never left my recollection. I hope my setting this down allows it to do so.

—B.C. Ahouse

#348 – Wednesday October 17, 2001

I have often experienced having someone hike or cut the price agreed upon in deal, whether buying or selling. On one occasion, I loaded a trailer full of shelled corn and the buyer reneged on the agreed price. I said, "OK, I'll flip you for it double or nothing. You flip and call." He lost and turned pale. I said, "Forget it, just pay the agreed price and leave."

On another occasion in building some houses in Painted Post, NY, the mafia sheetrock outfit my subcontractor hired tried to double the agreed price. I refused to listen. He said, "Fellow, we could do you in as a matter of business."

I said, "Sonny, I could kill you for the pleasure of it." He paid as agreed and left.

— B.C. Ahouse

#349 – Saturday October 20, 2001

My mother-in-law, Tillie "Brieker" "Lentz" "Olson", was a commendable woman in many ways except for her relationship with her two daughters, Irene and Peggy. I recall two incidents that exemplified Tillie's influence on Irene, my wife. Once while traveling south through Florida, it began raining heavily. We stopped in Daytona at dark and Irene called her mother to tell her we would be in on the morrow. Tillie said, "Don't you stay at a motel. Drive on tonight." We did and it ruined my eyes for a while (the headlight glare).

On another occasion, we got to Lake Worth early and instead of going to her mother's house, Irene had me drive around the cow pastures south and west of town to avoid getting to our destination early.

—B.C. Ahouse

#350 – Sunday October 21, 2001

About 30 years ago, I built a house on Sheldrake Point for a Thomas and Mary Tracey. A chance encounter yesterday with a man who was a member of the NYS Marine patrol reminded me of an incident that I related to him. There was a navigator's light buoy right of the point that was serviced by a crew in a motorboat. They removed the light bulb and then replaced it with a new one by holding them firmly and then slowly driving the boat around the buoy, first to remove and then to replace said bulbs. My new acquaintance said he believed me because the men were probably bored.

— B.C. Ahouse

#351 – Monday October 23, 2001

A few years ago, I became acquainted with a Dean Mitchell, who I met in Atlantic City. During our discussion, Dean confided to me that he was a Secret Service Agent and was on the left side of the car (running) when John F. Kennedy was shot. I later told him that he wasn't mentioned in the Warren Report. He told me that he was immediately sent out of the country for three years. This encounter reinforced my suspicions that the murder was carried out by three shooters, their last member being Lee Harvey Oswald, all of whom were dead ringers for each other. All know when Oswald was mentioned in police reports. I have no idea who Oswald was. Dean would not elaborate on this matter.

—B.C. Ahouse

#352 – Monday October 22, 2001

With all the discussion today after the tragedy of Sept. 11, 01, of the many the religions prevalent in their country and the freedom as such and the suppose separation from the U.S. government, it is worthy to consider as a fact that the U.S. government designated all the *** to the country has been supporting a religious cult—the State of Israel. It is basically a religious culture, not a conglomeration of Egyptian Jews and Khazur Jews. I am prompted to recall that our great President Theodore Roosevelt took it upon himself to publicly declare that the U.S. was a Christian nation. Basically because it was founded and mainly created by Christians. That is a solid consideration to be built upon.

—B.C. Ahouse

#353 – Tuesday October 23, 2001

Irene and I have four children: Karl (57), Martin (47), Susan (55), and Nancy (51). They have all been married: Karl twice, Martin once, Susan twice, and Nancy once. Although I have mentioned them in these memoirs separately, I have not discussed or tried to influence their marriages over the years for the simple reason I did not believe they would listen to me, or if they did it would have done any good. They are all in fairly good health and are happy. Irene is more inclined to help them financially than I, but I do somewhat too. Their mistakes, if any, are their own and my attitude leaves me free of any guilt, as long as abstinence is not a guilt.

—B.C. Ahouse

#354 – Thursday October 25, 2001

While at Ft. Belvoir, VA in 1942-43, I attended several lectures on Army indoctrination, and I recall two very interesting topics. Once, while being grilled on the merits and consequences of the war, I asked a major speaking if he could briefly tell us what the war was all about. He said it was about an ocean of oil in Arabia. Another time while discussing the Japs conduct during the Bataan March, a colonel related that he recently had retired as a liaison officer in Japan and told of an occasion in Mauchcke when a column of Jap infantry was pointed out as being on a march into their third day. He said, "My god, when do they sleep?" He was told they already knew how to sleep—so much for the treatment of their own troops.

— B.C. Ahouse

#355 – Friday October 26, 2001

With Halloween coming up shortly, I was reminded of a little ditty my father taught me about 75 years ago to say as a treat (or trick) while we were out Halloweening. It goes like this:

> *I had a little monkey*
> *I kept him in the country*
> *I feed him on charcoal bread*
> *Charcoal – Charcoal*
> *Fire up his asshole*
> *Now my monkey's dead*

Regardless to say it always got a big kick from adults hearing it from a couple little kids.

However, since charcoal is carcinogenous and colon cancer is a fear, the prophecy of these lyrics is ironic.

—B.C. Ahouse

#356 – Friday October 26, 2001

When I was a young fellow and first saw movies of Muslims kneeling in a mosque almost in formation, I thought they looked like a bunch of puppets. Not that I knew anything about their religion. Anyway, as the world has moved forward, it almost seems that my first impression was not very far from being correct. Events today almost convince me that these people are easily maneuvered and categorized in the image of the most provocative and aggressive leader, whether they adhere to their Koran teaching or not. Black American Muslims are in protest of their only hope — American Freedom.

—B.C. Ahouse

#357 – Sunday October 28, 2001

About 20 years ago while in White Plains, NY to address some legal business with a New York legal review attorney, Irene and I stayed at the Stauffers in White Plains. We also had dinner at the Stauffers restaurant adjoining the motel in a separate building. Irene remarked about the dumb layout of the area, which was difficult to get through. We were seated to the rear on a raised area that was isolated by a high fence with a narrow entrance. I said to Irene, "I'd hate to be in here if the place caught on fire." As fate had it, it did a day or so later, and 30 or so people died in the blaze. Ironically, a man who had just survived the MGM Hotel fire in Las Vegas also survived this incident as I recall.

— B.C. Ahouse

#358 – Monday October 29, 2001

In 1976, I was in Honolulu for the National Conservation Convention. A few of us had our dinner at the Royal Hawaiian Hotel restaurant next to the Sheraton, where we were staying. I had my first taste of Tia Maria that night. A few days later I was in the Seaport Inn in Lafina, Maui with Rod Sellers for dinner. He ordered Tia Maria as an after-dinner drink. When it was served in the usual small glasses, he sampled it and recalled the waitress to say it was not Tia Maria but Kaluha. She said it definitely was Tia Maria. Rod insisted it wasn't. She sent the bartender over, who tasted it. He said, "You are right. I'll make it right." He sent over a full bottle of Tia Maria with two large glasses and said enjoy. That was the same night and place I met Francis Ford Coppola, who invited me to Hollywood for a screen test. I didn't go. Irene wouldn't have believed me.

— B.C. Ahouse

#359 – Monday October 29, 2001

Some years ago, old Mr. Hurlbert the funeral director and undertaker in Interlaken, NY, came into Hank Green's barber shop in the same village and said he had just read something that he couldn't keep quiet about. It was a letter in Dear Abby's column from a lady who had just married a mortician and was quite concerned about their connubial relations. It seemed from her letter that before her husband would have sex with her, he insisted that she take a cold soaking bath and lay perfectly still while he preformed his husbandly duties. Mr. Hurlbert wouldn't explain his opinion, but everyone else in the shop did.

—B.C. Ahouse

#360 – Tuesday October 30, 2001

My friend Carl Ahner, who was also my Corporal at the Engineer Replacement Training Center at Ft. Belvoir, VA, was a pleasure to know and visit with. He was from Limestone Road, Delaware and often talked about his family and experiences. I recall the fact that his father was an advocate of the deceased preacher Billy Sunday, who had a collection of his sermons on Victrola records. Carl often told of how Billy Sunday usually began his sermons by advising all the ladies present to close their legs and close the gates to Hell. The last time I saw Carl was on the street in Washington, D.C. after a snowstorm while Irene was on her way back to NYC. Carl admonished me to get rated for disability before I had left the Army, but I didn't.

—B.C. Ahouse

#361 – Wednesday October 31, 2001

About 45 years ago, Irene's mother Tillie Lentz had recently married John Olson from Hancock, Michigan—a fine Finnish fellow. We were invited to visit them at the cottage on Portage Lake. Our whole family was given the grand tour of the copper country. While up at Copper Harbor, the extreme north of the area, we stopped at a lookout with a great view. As we were enjoying the scenery, someone's car lost its brakes and ran down the parking lot slope and over the cliff. A fellow next to us said some fool didn't set his brakes properly, whereupon his wife said, "Hey that was our car." Probably with this in mind, John gave me some unedited advice: never pull out in front of an old car.

—B.C. Ahouse

#362 – Friday November 2, 2001

The night I was in the Provost Marshall's office in Ft. Belvoir with Sam Savitts, Warren Pershing and Pete Dailey, Pete got talking about the White House, since his father "he said" was FDR's private chauffeur. He reflected on Eleanor's leftist leanings but then elaborated on FDR's extramarital affair with a long-standing partner who usually accompanied him to *** Spring, Georgia, where he eventually died with her in presence. I related this to Irene's mother, who put me down, saying our president would never do any such thing. However, many years later this situation became public and scandalized the memories of Franklin Delano Roosevelt.

— B.C. Ahouse

#363 – Friday November 2, 2001

My granddaughter Laura Louise Warren (who was just married last Saturday 10-27-01 to Richard Hill VI of Savona, NY), when a teenager, used to baby-sit a young blonde boy (a neighbor in Savona). This boy, Derrick Robie, was murdered by a young friend, Eric Smith, who lured Derrick into a woodlot (which Laura used to walk by on her way to school) and choked him to death. Needless to say, this traumatized the community, especially after details were known. Apparently, Eric Smith was labeled a victim himself (child neglect and abuse). I never heard of his trial and reversal and as Laura told me recently, he was in a prison facility.

—B.C. Ahouse

#364 – Saturday November 3, 2001

Early in 1976, I was on my way to the Syracuse Airport—Irene driving on her way to a spa. The car broke down in Waterloo. A piece of the exhaust pipe came loose and fouled the emissions. We had another car brought up and made it to the airport but too late for my flight. When we were renewing my ticket, the attendant made it out for two people, but Irene wouldn't fly and went on her own way. I finally got to Honolulu for the NACD Convention, after which I and Rod Sellers decided to go further. When I applied for the additional ticket, the clerk said, "Let me see your ticket," and accepted it. He did and in examining my ticket he said, "This is for two people. I owe you $600.00." I explained the error and he then eliminated the two-person item. Later it dawned on me—did he pocket the $600.00?

—B.C. Ahouse

#365 – Monday November 5, 2001

Since Irene has become incapacitated, I am becoming somewhat of a cook. So, I recall a few incidents. In 1947, I dug up some horseradish roots by the Peterson House. I cleaned them, ground them up as directed and closed them up in a couple of jars. When I took the lid off, a cloud of very acrid smoke erupted. Also, about that time, Irene's friend Evelyn Doir was with her husband, a British merchantman who introduced us to stewed bacon and tomatoes and his favorite, Bubbley squash. During my hunting trips to New Albany, PA, Clarence Hatch gave me his secret for his famous hunters stew. Start out with some sautéed beef. Use all and any vegetables, rice, barley etc. and simmer for hours. When thoroughly cooked, add and stir in a bottle of ketchup and a pound of butter—voilà!

—B.C. Ahouse

#366 – Monday November 5, 2001

To reflect on some of my opinions on highway problems, once when in NYC visiting our daughter Susan, I was annoyed by the constant unnecessary horn blowing. While going across the block on 14th Street where Sue lived, I stopped for a stop sign and the car behind me needlessly sounded the horn constantly and loud. I got out of the car, went to the driver and asked him if he needed help or anything. He looked dumb and said, "Mister, you taught me something." Regarding those steel shrouds that are supposedly guardrails, about 1974 going into Painted Post, NY, I saw a car hit them. They broke loose and the steel came into the car, killing the driver. Also a Father Mike, a priest who prayed for Irene in Geneva General Hospital in 1994, was killed by the same steel shroud going into Corning to visit his mother when he fell asleep.

—B.C. Ahouse

#367 – Monday November 5, 2001

With all the concern today on TV about breast cancer, I recalled an incident when I was operating a dairy here in Lodi probably 50 years ago. We always washed down the cows' udders before milking, and on one occasion I noticed a hot spot on the center of the side of the cow's udder. When I pressed it with my finger, it penetrated the bag and a black mess oozed out. There was no previous symptom here. Another time, I was working our farm in Schuyler County on the corner of the Searsburg Road and Logen Road. A county roadwork crew had stopped for lunch at the Peach Tree Creek Bridge. I wandered over to visit, and in the discussion this young fellow mentioned a pain in his shinbone. I asked him how tender it was. He pressed it and his finger went into it a good inch—cancer. He lost his leg.

—B.C. Ahouse

And so ends the first 367 entries in Bernie's memoir. This volume was transcribed from handwritten notes, whose quality gradually deteriorated as the months wore on. In order to complete this as a surprise for Bernie on his 90th birthday, literary liberty was taken where questions in the transcript were evident.

More than a hundred pages in his own handwriting remain un-transcribed due to illegibility. We hope to sit with Bernie after this edition is presented to fill in the blanks in these first 367 entries and begin to sort through the final hundred or so pages.

We hope to print a definitive, second edition of the memoir, including images and scanned additions from Bernie's collection, at a later date... but we need Bernie's help for that.

www.ingramcontent.com/pod-product-compliance
Lightning Source LLC
Chambersburg PA
CBHW031824090426
42741CB00005B/128